STEP-BY-STEP GARDEN GUIDES

Siegfried Stein

Propagation

AURA

Step-by-Step Garden Guides Propagation

Siegfried Stein

German-language edition and photographs
*Gärtnern leicht und richtig
Aussaat und Vermehrung*
© 1994 BLV Verlagsgesellschaft mbH, München

English-language edition
© 1995 Transedition Ltd,
Oxford OX4 4DJ, England

Translation: Andrew Shackleton/Asgard Publishing Services
Editing: Asgard Publishing Services, Leeds
Typesetting:
Organ Graphic, Abingdon

Photographic credits
All photographs by the author except:
Eisenbeiss 73; Photos Horticultural front cover, 4, 14, 56 tr, 88, 89; Harry Smith 27, 66 br; Thompson & Morgan 20

This edition published by
Aura Books plc

10 9 8 7 6 5 4
Printed in Dubai

ISBN 0 947793 75 5

Contents

Everything you need for your plant nursery

Propagating your own plants is an enjoyable and highly creative activity.

It may be that you're taking cuttings from an ageing geranium to produce new blooms, or perhaps you're just sowing a bed of summer flowers. Simply seeing the plants grow and flourish is a pleasure in itself.

It's also worth remembering that propagating plants for yourself can save you a lot of money — and the larger your garden, the tighter your budget is likely to be.

The first essential: getting the soil right

Some cuttings take root very easily — all you need is a jar of fresh water.

Others may need a propagating medium made up of one part clean sharp sand to one part finely divided peat (or a peat substitute such as cocoa fibre). Your home-made mixture should be low in nutrients: this will stimulate root growth as the plant searches for food.

Alternatively you could use one of the many commercially available seed or propagating composts. You want a loosely structured medium that is porous and well ventilated without being powdery; as we've said, it should be low in nutrients, but it should also have enough lime to bring its pH up to about 5.5-6.5.

Even after you've sieved it, your home-made seed compost will still contain many moulds and bacteria. Some of these could easily damage your seedlings, so you should always sterilise your compost before you actually use it.

You can do this by wrapping it up in some kind of heat-resistant material, and putting it in an oven pre-heated to 300°F (150°C) for half an hour. Alternatively you can put it in a microwave oven rated at 600 W for 10-15 minutes at full power (adjust the time for other wattages).

The right equipment

Your **seed trays** shouldn't be too deep, as this can make pricking out difficult.

A selection of pots and trays suitable for use in propagation.

Suitable pots

Peat Jiffy pots — tablets that swell up and turn into little pots — are particularly suitable for members of the cucumber family. These plants need to develop a root ball before they are planted out, or else their sensitive roots can easily be damaged.

Plastic **yoghurt pots** are popular seeding containers and don't cost a thing. Cardboard **egg boxes** have the added advantage that they are biodegradable.

Recycled paper pots are designed so that they break down in the soil to form humus. Don't worry if you find they're covered with an ugly-looking mould. This is normal with organic materials, and completely harmless. However, you should never allow the recycled paper to dry out. Tear open the pot when you plant out, so the roots get as much direct contact with the soil as possible — this will help them to grow.

Propagating tools

These are equally important, and should normally include the following:

- a well-sharpened knife, scalpel or razor-blade for taking cuttings
- plastic dibbers
- plant labels and a suitably weatherproof writing implement (there are special pencils for this)

No need to throw your pots away: peat Jiffy pots can simply be planted out together with your plants.

- a sieve (quite essential when you're growing plants from seed)
- a collection of large glass tumblers and/or plastic bags to help create a humid micro-climate that will encourage the growth of your young plants
- a spray or watering can with a fine rose that won't flood the plantlets.
- an indoor thermometer

Make sure your watering can is big enough for the work you will be doing with it — and if you are using tap water, always let it stand for a while before using it.

A long spout can be very helpful (or at least one that's long enough to reach the centre of your largest plant). A plant sprayer is also very useful: sometimes a fine mist is the most effective way of providing water for your plants, and for maintaining the high humidity that is often so important for propagation.

It doesn't matter how old your tools are, as long as they can do the job you want them to do. The important thing is to look after them properly, and to keep them scrupulously clean at all times. This will remove any risk of transferring pests or diseases from one plant to another.

It also avoids the risk that plants such as oleander and *Dieffenbachia* may leave poisonous substances on your tools. If a tool isn't cleaned after you've finished with it, there's a chance you could transfer these substances to your eyes or your mouth, where they could cause a very unpleasant inflammation. If you have sensitive skin, your hands may be equally vulnerable.

Most cuttings have no trouble forming roots. However, citrus plants, camellias and woody tub plants will need a little help from an appropriate hormone preparation. There are a number of suitable **rooting powders** on the market. Dip the cut end of the cutting into the rooting powder, shake off the excess, and put the cutting in your propagating compost.

Young plants need warmth and moisture

If you're trying to propagate plants at home, you will find that young plants can only germinate and develop properly if they are kept warm enough. It's true that most plants will flourish at room temperature (i.e. 64-72°F; 18-22°C), but there are a number of exceptions to this.

Cabbage lettuce germinates better when it's kept at about 46-54°F (8-12°C). Temperatures over 64-68°F (18-20°C) interfere with germination, which is very poor in hot summers. To deal with this problem, wrap your seeds in a damp cloth, keep them in the fridge for 24 hours to pre-germinate before sowing, and sow only in the evening.

Some seeds (such as violets, primulas, spring adonis and sweet woodruff) need cool, damp, winter-like conditions if they are going to overcome their natural inhibitors and germinate properly (for a fuller explanation see page 40).

However, most plants germinate best at room temperature, or in the temperatures you would normally find outdoors in May — i.e. at around 64-68°F (18-20°C). Plants that prefer warmth, such as cucumbers, peppers and melons, need a temperature of at least

72°F (22°C) — and preferably 77°F (25°C) — to germinate readily.

If cuttings or seeds are particularly sensitive, they may benefit from a little localised heat. For this you can use a low-voltage hotplate, heating cables in the soil or a propagator that's equipped with a temperature control.

High humidity is equally vital for successful germination. If

Beans that have been propagated indoors will escape the unwelcome attentions of the bean fly.

the surrounding air isn't humid enough, the plant tissues won't develop. You can increase the humidity level by using an automatic spray or an electric humidifier, and you can maintain humidity by covering your seedbed with fleece or growing

6

BASICS

film, or by putting glass over your cuttings to stop them drying out. In these conditions your plants will readily germinate and start to grow.

One helpful and inexpensive solution is to use a home propagator. This consists of a plastic tray with a transparent lid, usually vented to stop the plants rotting.

An even simpler method than this is to put the seed tray in a large transparent plastic bag, or to lay plastic sheeting over the top of the seed tray. Plants protected in this way won't dry out, but they'll need fresh air as soon as they have germinated or they'll start to rot. This type of propagator is also useful for rooting soft tip cuttings (see page 53).

Light and shade

Light is a plant's main energy source. This, combined with the water and nutrients it takes up through its roots, and the carbon dioxide in the air, is what the plant needs to create new tissue.

Different plants have different requirements for light, but there's a minimum level below which growth is impossible. This is around 800-1,000 lux (the normal unit of measurement for light).

The light levels on a bright summer's day can often be as high as 150,000-200,000 lux. In December, on the other hand, there may be as little as 1,500-2,000 lux, and even less

will come through a window. Dull, cloudy days when there are fewer hours of daylight can be a problem for plants. They quickly become stunted and prone to disease. To produce healthier growth they're almost certainly going to need an additional source of light.

During the winter — i.e. from the beginning of December through to early March — it's sensible to arrange some additional lighting for about 10-12 hours a day.

There's a wide choice of suitable lamps on the market, including some that produce a particular kind of red light that encourages growth. Some lamps are specially waterproofed like aquarium lights.

Double fluorescent tubes (with a shade to direct the light downward) should be placed about 1 ft (30 cm) above the plants. About 40-60 W/m^2 is

normally enough to encourage the development of vegetables or summer flowers. It also stops the plantlets growing too fast, which will make them weak and leggy.

From March onwards the natural levels of light will be enough to encourage plenty of growth. Don't sow too early: nature will soon make up for any delays. Tomatoes and peppers, in particular, don't need more than 7-8 weeks to grow from seed into fully mature plants. If you sow them too early, the plants will grow too long and weak; you want them to be sturdy and stocky as they grow. Give them plenty of fresh air, either outdoors or through an open window, to help them harden up properly.

Supplementary lighting will promote growth during the dullest winters.

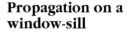

Direct sunlight can sometimes burn your plants. Too much heat could make the leaves wilt. All young plants do nicely in a well-lit position that isn't in direct sunlight, or in partial shade (under a sheet of newspaper, for instance). Well-ventilated, permeable fleece can also be very effective. So can slitted plastic sheeting (also known as growing film).

In general you'll find that seeds will germinate most successfully when the thickness of soil that covers them is no more than three or four times the size of the seed. The uppermost layer of the soil is rich in oxygen, and this is a vital factor in the processes of rooting and germination.

Nearly all seeds germinate in the dark, but there are several notable exceptions. These include many of the herbs (for example, valerian, basil, thyme, chamomile and hyssop) and a few ornamentals such as busy Lizzie (*Impatiens*). With these plants you simply press the seeds into the earth and moisten them. Use only the thinnest layer of soil, if any, to cover them — or, if you prefer, you can cover them with newspaper to create a sort of artificial twilight. This will produce the right kind of conditions for the germinating seeds.

In many plants the growth phase — the time when you can propagate them — is determined by the number of daylight hours that are available. Chrysanthemums, poinsettias and flaming Katy (*Kalanchoe*), for example, come into flower in the autumn. You should propagate them by June at the very latest (i.e. when the days are longest) — and if you insist on propagating them in the middle of the flowering period, you must use additional lighting to simulate longer days and produce the right reactions from the plant.

Propagation on a window-sill

Very few of our cultivated plants are actually native to western Europe. In fact, most of our flowers have come to us down the centuries from as far afield as China and Japan, travelling along the ancient trade routes through Persia, Greece and Italy. Later on the Spaniards opened up yet another supply from the New World. Many of these plants need to be cultivated under frost-free conditions.

Plants like these can be grown in a conservatory — or, if you wish, they can equally well be grown on a window-sill in a sunny room. There will invariably be problems of space, but you can overcome them with a propagator that's been designed for use in the home. Some designs will even fit on a window-sill. Others have a continuous watering system: the plants themselves draw the water they need from a fleece underlay, which is replenished automatically by a wick that goes down to a water storage tank underneath the propagator.

If you've got a radiator under the window-sill, there's no need to worry: it can provide the necessary heat for sensitive seeds or exotics, or for house or tub plants. Many such plants

Seedlings neatly housed in a home propagator.

can be raised from seed at very little expense. Among them are angel's trumpet (*Datura*), bananas, palms and even fuchsias.

A well-lit window-sill can also provide the ideal conditions for growing cuttings from window-box plants such as geraniums and fuchsias, from tub plants such as marguerites, citrus plants and oleander — and of course from pot plants.

You should always be very careful of deep window-sills. At first they may seem perfect for houseplants, offering all the space you could want. But there's a problem that becomes obvious when you think about it. Deep window-sills especially may be much colder than the rest of the room, and particularly on winter nights. At such times they're a lot closer to the cold air outside — and if you're like most people, you'll probably want to draw the curtains. This effectively insulates the window-sill from the warm air inside the room itself. The air can become quite cold out there, so if you think your window-sill could fit this description, check it out for yourself with a thermometer.

Propagation in a garden frame

Garden frames are less important these days than they used to be. The various modern films and fleeces are just as good for creating a suitable microclimate. These coverings

A garden frame is less trouble to build than a greenhouse, and provides plenty of space for new seedlings.

have another advantage, too: they'll let the rain get through to your plants. This means, of course, that you don't have to go out and water the plants specially.

Even so, garden frames can still prove extremely useful for propagating some of the less sensitive vegetables and summer flowers so that they're ready to be planted out in April or May.

They can also be used to propagate biennial flowers such as pansies, or to provide shelter for growing cucumbers, melons and aubergines in the summer, and leeks, chicory and dandelion roots in the winter.

Garden frames make the best place for sowing cold germinators (see page 40) such as anemones, primulas and violets. They are also well suited to growing shrubs and perennials from cuttings, or to making grafts that require extremely high humidity in order to take.

Whether you're trying to grow from hardwood or softwood cuttings, from runners or divided plants, they'll all take root under a garden frame. All you need to do is to put them in pots or troughs full of moist compost, give them a little shade and make sure they don't dry out.

Garden frames, like greenhouses, can be fitted with automatic vents. These are designed to open and shut automatically as the temperature rises and falls.

You can buy ready-made frames made of easy-care aluminium, plastic or wood, or alternatively you can build them yourself using wood, concrete slabs and sheets of horticultural glass.

Making things grow in a greenhouse

A small greenhouse is the ideal place to propagate and grow all kinds of plants. Whether it's heated or not, there's always a way to create the conditions that you need.

If a greenhouse is going to do its job properly, it must be in the right position. Never build it in the shade; try to find the sunniest position you can, and if possible choose a sheltered site that isn't too far away from the house.

The best orientation for a greenhouse is with the largest side facing southwards, so that the plants have the best chance to soak up warmth and sunlight. An easterly or westerly aspect is just about acceptable, but do try to avoid a northerly or shaded situation. And never build a greenhouse under a large tree (though you could use a small tree or a climber to provide some partial shade).

Choose the greenhouse design that you like best, and which is most suitable for your needs. If the roof is steeply angled and facing towards the sun, you could even install a solar heating system for your home, which could eventually give you a considerable saving on your heating bills.

A sunken greenhouse will also save a lot of energy, because the side walls are effectively insulated from the air outside. While there won't be enough light coming in for you to grow

vegetables inside, it will provide the ideal microclimate for orchids.

There's quite a vogue in some circles for hexagonal or octagonal greenhouses with elaborate curved or angular roofs. These structures may be very attractive to look at, but they are

expensive in comparison to the amount of the useful space that they provide. You'll also need to find out whether they come equipped with suitably shaped tables, storage surfaces, hanging areas and roof ventilation — and preferably at an affordable price.

Here are a few general points that you will probably need to be thinking about when you start looking out for a suitable greenhouse:

• Make sure the doors open outwards, or slide, and that they're wide enough to allow

a wheelbarrow to pass in and out as easily as possible.

• What is the greenhouse made of? Wooden structures are attractive and natural-looking, but you have to work much harder to maintain them. They must be cleaned and

painted regularly, and they have a relatively limited lifespan. These days aluminium alloy structures have effectively become the norm.

• Make sure there are no sharp edges that you (or your children) could injure yourself on, either on the greenhouse structure itself or on any of the installations.

• The structure should be well made; it should fit together snugly, without leaving any gaps in the framework that could let in cold air.

• The various secondary elements like staging (benches), shelves, hooks and blinds should be straightforward to install or remove.

• Choose a design that uses the largest possible panes of glass. Small, overlapping panes are difficult to keep clean, and also tend to be rather leaky.

• Whether your greenhouse is made of glass, rigid plastic or polythene sheeting will depend on how large it is and on what you can afford. In general, all three of these materials can provide effective protection for growing plants — though glass is certainly the best.

With tub plants, seedlings and pottings-on, this greenhouse is full of plants at different stages of development.

11

Polythene, fleece, tunnels and netting

At first your cuttings have no roots at all, which means they have only a very limited ability to replace any moisture that they lose through evaporation. As a result, anything that you can do to reduce evaporation by increasing the humidity of the air around them is going to improve their chances, and is bound to improve the results that you obtain. Apart from regular spaying, the best way to achieve this improved microclimate is to protect your plantlets with some kind of transparent or translucent structure. Even inside a greenhouse, this may still be a very good idea. It will create a separate chamber in which you can set up exactly the right kind of conditions for your new plants.

The best solution for propagating young plants in the open air

Conditions under this fleece are highly favourable to growth.

Strawberries ripen much more quickly under plastic film.

is a **tunnel construction** made of stretched polythene pierced with holes or slits. A tunnel like this can easily be put together from ready-made (and readily available) parts. However, it's important to provide ventilation for your plants if they're going to be exposed to strong sunshine. Wind can be a problem, too, because it's impossible to make a tunnel completely draught-proof.

If you're only propagating a few plants, then an upturned jam jar may be quite enough. Other cheap alternatives include a plastic bag pierced with a few ventilation holes, or even some clingfilm from the kitchen.

Another option is to use **fleece**, a translucent, extremely lightweight fabric that is normally coloured white. This new product from the textile industry is being used for many gardening jobs, and can be stretched over a table, a seed tray or even a garden frame. Fleece helps to speed up plant growth, and provides a certain amount of shade at the same time. It also allows air to pass through virtually unhindered, so it doesn't reduce water loss through evaporation. Even so, fleece is still extremely useful for protecting young perennials, shrubs and conifers, or seedlings and pricked-out plantlets against wind and other adverse conditions. It's particularly useful with plants that have already formed roots, since with these the only thing you need to worry about is making them grow faster.

Garden netting is a strong plastic mesh that will normally last for years. Its main purpose is to protect plants from bird damage, but fine-meshed netting can also be effective against insect infestations. It will, for example, prevent the cabbage white butterfly from laying its eggs on your vegetables, which might otherwise fall victim to the voracious appetites of its hatching caterpillars. Netting, like fleece, provides a consider-able amount of shelter from the wind, and so helps to produce a favourable microclimate.

There are several ways of installing netting. You *can* just lay it over your plants and anchor it all around with pegs or bags of soil. But there is a more elegant solution: stretch-ing it over wire arches to form a tunnel. The tunnel will help to protect your growing plants against wind and pests, but that is not all. You can also put par-ticularly sensitive cuttings and seedlings in their own propaga-tors inside the tunnel, and thus kill two birds with one stone.

Netting has proved extremely effective in plant propagation. It protects the young plants per-fectly, and if you take care of it properly it should last you four to five years. You can even wash it to remove any dirt that has collected on it.

Hygiene is vital

This is logical if you think about it. Even adult plants can suc-cumb to attacks from a whole

variety of pests and diseases. New cuttings have no roots and are clearly weak and vulnerable, so they're wide open to attack.

Start right at the beginning, with the parent plant. Look after it carefully and give it plenty of light so it'll be in the best poss-ible condition when you take cuttings from it; and make sure it isn't carrying any pests or dis-eases that could be passed on.

If you want your cuttings to take root fast, and you want to avoid infestations, then you'll need to work quickly and hygienically. Pests, and any kind of disease — fungal, viral or bacterial — will do far more damage to weakened plants. Don't give them a chance to attack. Make sure the knife or razor-blade that you use is sterile. Just passing it through a candle flame immediately before cutting is a simple procedure that you can rely on to reduce any danger of infection.

The large tray provides protection against slugs, while the netting wards off a variety of insect pests.

Always use pots, trays and other tools made from materials that are easy to clean and dis-infect. In most cases this will mean plastic.

Make sure your working area is clean, too. If you're working with a particularly important plant, or you're planning to carry out a whole series of tasks, then it's worth taking the extra trouble to give the whole area a thorough scrubbing. Use a good household disinfectant.

Finally, it goes almost without saying that the compost or propagation medium that you intend to use should be both clean and fresh. Any soil that has already been used is likely to be contaminated — it should be consigned to the compost heap, where it's less likely to do any harm.

13

The main pests and diseases

Diseases of propagation

A number of fungal infections with exotic names such as *Pythium*, *Rhizoctonia* and *Thilavia* are the direct result of propagating in unfavourable or unhygienic conditions, e.g. when plants don't get enough light, or they are kept too moist, or they become too crowded. These infections produce areas of soft, brown rotting tissue. If the shoots remain too soft and fail to ripen, then they are similarly vulnerable. The cuttings or seedlings collapse, either within rows or across whole areas.

You should treat the disease as soon as you find it, because the infection will spread fast. Spray the plants with a suitable fungicide, then keep them well ventilated.

Grey mould (*Botrytis cinerea*)

This disease is common world-wide, and will attack any plant that is weakened, damaged, crowded or standing in soil that is too wet. The damage can be considerable, with rotting leaves and shoots. Move the plant into brighter, drier conditions, and treat it with a fungicide.

The herbs in the tray on the right have been kept too moist; as a result they are falling victim to a fungal infection. Compare the healthy plants in the central tray.

Viral infections

Many ornamental plants are vulnerable to viral infections, especially geraniums, roses, chrysanthemums and pinks. The visible symptoms include distorted leaves and shoots, and light-coloured, unhealthy-looking stripes or spots on the leaves and flowers. Plant growth is invariably poor.

Never take cuttings from affected plants. This is not only useless but dangerous, too: the viruses are spread by contact or injury. Any affected plant that you find should be put in the dustbin at once — never put it on the compost heap, or you risk further infection later on.

There are unfortunately no cures for viral infections. Modern horticulturalists simply go back to the laboratory and look for some fresh, unaffected plant tissue from which to propagate a new generation of healthy plants.

Viruses are often spread by a variety insect pests (see below), so you should take care to keep these under control on vulnerable plants.

Pests

First make sure your parent plants are free of any pests and diseases. Any problems of this kind must be treated before propagation begins.

14

Even after that, you should always keep a careful watch for any signs of infestation, and deal with it at once.

Aphids

Among the best-known of this family of plant pests is the familiar greenfly. Aphids breed amazingly fast. Tell-tale signs of an infestation include leaves and shoots sticking together or becoming distorted. However, they can be easily dealt with using insecticides and various biological controls.

Snails and slugs

These common garden animals can be as much of a plague in greenhouses as they are in the open air. They are often carried in with soil or moss. They cause considerable damage, devouring leaves, roots and shoots alike with gusto.

The best method of control is to lure them away with a tasty meal of fresh potato peelings left out for them overnight. In the morning you can take the animals away.

Woodlice

These creatures can be dealt with the same way. They live on soft plant tissue, and sometimes cause damage to roots or freshly cut stems.

Fungus gnats

The adult insects lay black-coloured eggs 1 in (2-3 mm) long in damp soil. The white maggots that emerge feed on rotting vegetation, and devour roots and tubers. You can fight

them by watering the soil with a biological control preparation that contains nematodes of the genus *Steinernema*.

Whiteflies

This infestation can be controlled by hanging up traps made of yellow card covered in a sticky substance; proprietary traps are easy to find. You can also control whitefly biologically with *Encarsia formosa*.

Red spider mites

These annoying pests don't normally develop in the humid

You can avoid mildew by making sure that your plants aren't over-crowded.

conditions that are necessary for propagation. They, too, can be controlled biologically by introducing predatory mites called *Phytoseilus*.

Scale insects

Scale insects are usually introduced from an affected parent plant. However, you can get rid of them very easily by simply wiping them off.

15

Everything starts from seed

Plants have one important advantage over many other living things: they can reproduce both sexually (by means of flowers, seeds and pollination) and asexually (by means of cuttings, runners, tubers, bulbs, division and root cuttings).

Plants have many different ways of attracting insects for **pollination**, including fragrant scents and attractive flowers; some plants, like *Arum*, will even trap the insect inside the flower. The purpose of using insects is to spread the pollen to the stigmas of other flowers, which ensures a healthy genetic mix. Some grasses (e.g. maize), together with spinach, oak and hazel, use the wind to spread their pollen. Pondweed (*Elodea*) makes use of water currents.

Some plants are what is known as **self-pollinating**. They include peas, beans, tomatoes, aubergines, sweet peas, lupins, oranges and figs. In most cases (e.g. the sunflower) the male organs (the stamens and anthers) and female organs (carpels and stigmas) are found close together on the same flower. Sometimes the two are well apart but still on the same plant, as with maize, cucumbers, melons, pumpkins and castor-oil plants. But in just a few cases (e.g. spinach, olives and sea buckthorn) each plant is either exclusively male or exclusively female.

A selection of leguminous fruits from the pea and bean family

The more successful the pollination, the better the resulting crop. Poor pollination (e.g. in tomatoes and aubergines) often leads to misshapen fruit.

Give your aubergine or tomato flowers a shake at around midday, when air humidity is relatively low. This will make sure the pollen reaches the stigma in time, and you'll be certain of a good, healthy crop.

Summer bedding being grown for seed in the sunny plains of central California.

The **seed** is produced by the fruit cells. It contains genetic information (genes) derived from both the male and the female parts of the parent plants. It is the genes that determine such factors as the plant's size, growth habit, flower colour, fruit shape, scent, fertility and resistance to disease. The seed also contains stores of energy in the form of carbohydrates (glucose and starch), fats, vitamins and trace elements that will give it a start in life.

These various elements will enable it to germinate, and to survive the first growth phase until the roots start to bring in water and nutrients from the soil, and the leaves take over the role of producing plant tissue. Enzymes are released as the seed swells, and light, warmth, air and moisture are absorbed. Then the starch stored in the seed turns into glucose, which provides the energy for germination.

You can watch this process going on. The seed case bursts, and the seed germ appears with the cotyledons (seed leaves) and embryonic roots already forming. Some flowering plants — notably grasses (including maize), palms, lilies and orchids — produce only one cotyledon, and are therefore known as **monocotyledons**. Most other flowering plants are **dicotyledons**, and have two seed leaves. When the first proper leaves appear, the process of germination is complete.

Basic genetic theory

Charles Darwin (1809–82) explained the process of natural selection, whereby only the best-adapted individuals survive to continue the species. But it was an abbot named Gregor. Mendel (1822–84) working in Moravia who explained the regular processes of genetic inheritance in plants.

The sexual reproduction of plants was understood before Mendel began his experiments, but no one understood the principles of natural heredity. As a result, breeding and hybridisation were seen as completely random processes.

Mendel experimented with pea plants and four o'clock flowers (*Mirabilis jalapa*). He discovered that if you cross a white-flowered plant with a red-flowered one, then all the plants created from pure-bred parents will have pink flowers. What's more, a similar pattern can be observed when you study other features of the same plants.

The products of this direct form of hybridisation (i.e. from a single successful cross) are known as F1 hybrids (from the Latin *filia*, meaning 'daughter'). Such hybrids are generally more

17

vigorous than both the parent strains, having stronger growth, more flowers and fruit, and greater resistance to disease.

If F1 hybrids are to be successful, the parent strains must be carefully bred for specific genes and tested for their suitability as partners. Where long pedigrees with known genes exist, plant breeders can try out new combinations. For instance, they might combine the disease-resistance of wild plants with the beauty of some cultivated strains so that spraying becomes unnecessary.

However, if you try to propagate from the seeds of these F1 hybrids, the genes will be dispersed and you won't be able to produce consistently pure-bred offspring. So it's no use sowing the seeds of F1 hybrids.

If you want to breed such plants from seed, then — like all plant breeders — you should adhere strictly to the principle of Mendel's second law. After you've created a successful F1 hybrid, the genes will be distributed among the generations that follow according to a specific numerical pattern. The art of successful breeding is to recognise and select the specific genetic combination that you want, to reject the many undesirable combinations, and to follow this process through several generations until you eventually produce a single pure-bred variety (or **cultivar**) that can be propagated successfully from seed. The whole process can take anything between 10 and 20 years, depending on whether

Modern plant varieties grow more compactly than the species or older varieties.

the flowers, fruits and seeds develop in the first year after seeding or only after overwintering (as in the case of carrots).

That's not all. Many genes appear according to a somewhat more unequal pattern. Often a particular gene in one of the parent plants proves to be dominant, and effectively masks the corresponding gene in the other parent (the recessive gene) even when both are present.

Many plant breeders, whether they're amateurs or professionals, simply don't have the time or the patience to spend many years creating a pure-bred variety. They prefer to use the successful hybrid straight away, propagating it asexually by means of division, layering, cuttings, bulbs or tubers.

Modern horticulturalists have moved this process into the laboratory, where they can now create many new plants from a culture containing just a few cells taken from the **meristem** (growth tissue) of a single parent plant. This so-called meristematic tissue is found only in certain parts of the plant such as the shoot tips, roots, buds, anthers and stigma. Strictly speaking the products of this propagation method are clones: all of them are genetically identical.

One result of these new techniques is that some plants (e.g. rare orchid strains) that were once difficult and expensive to reproduce can now be propagated relatively cheaply and quickly. High-quality strawberries and valuable shrubs can also be made available at reasonable prices.

Plant breeding at home

It is always possible to breed your own plant strains, trying out new and interesting combinations to produce new colours, shapes and other features. It's not unusual, it's perfectly legal, and it isn't particularly difficult. Many good plant strains are the long-term result of clever thinking and insight on the part of individual gardeners.

If you're interested in breeding a particular kind of plant, there are special-interest groups and societies for roses, lilies, perennials, cacti, orchids and fuchsias (to name but a few). Here you can find out more about your particular plants, and form links for the exchange (or perhaps even the sale) of new and successful strains.

All you need to create a new hybrid is a small paintbrush or a pair of tweezers for transferring pollen, two good parent plants and the necessary knowledge for the task. It's worth noting, however, that hybrids can normally be created only within a species. Exceptions to this, such as hybrids between certain *Brassica* species, are by their very nature unusual.

Collecting your seed

At one time it was quite customary for gardeners to harvest their own seed for the next sowing. Even today, there are plant enthusiasts who like to collect their own seed, and there are also many plant species that will self-seed quite readily for themselves.

This isn't always an advantage, however. Pansies, for example, if left to their own devices, quickly revert to flowers of mixed colours that are visibly smaller; and if you sow bean seed from your own harvest, they will carry on any transferable diseases such as leaf spot, which will be impossible to eradicate the following year.

Such risks can be minimised by scrupulous breeding. Bean seed, for example, is produced commercially in East Africa, where the disease cycle is interrupted by the regular alternation between rain during the growing period and drought during the ripening period.

So there are advantages in always buying fresh seed for each new crop.

In any case, breeding from F1 hybrids is doomed from the start, and many species are pollinated by insects, which tend to bring in unwanted strains from neighbouring gardens. Carrots, cabbages, spinach beet and parsley are all biennial vegetables, so they're hardly worth the

effort. And in the case of cress, spinach and cabbage lettuce the seed is so cheap to buy that you have to be really interested if you're going to bother using your own seed.

If you do decide to harvest your own seed, here are some tips. Let the seed ripen fully on the plant. Then harvest it on a dry, sunny day from fully ripened, dried-out pods or umbels; you can tell if they're ripe from the brown colour of the seeds.

Flower clusters that grow skywards should, if necessary, be protected from rain. Fruits such as tomatoes, cucumbers and melons should be allowed to ripen fully before the seeds are finally extracted, then washed and dried.

Dry the seed out on a rack, in a box or hung up in a porous bag, in a dry, well-ventilated place that's protected from rain, fog and other humidity. Keep it there until the late autumn or winter, when it's time for the next part of the process.

Now at last you can remove the seed from its pod, capsule or flower-head. You can usually manage this simply by rubbing it between the palms of your hands, or by beating it with a pestle. Use a sieve to separate the seed from the chaff, and then to wash it clean.

All you need is an ordinary household colander to separate the wheat from the chaff.

19

Seed quality and germination tests

The seeds of vegetables and other important crop species are subject to strict controls. Samples must be tested to ensure that they fulfil the stipulated requirements for germination and purity of strain. That way buyers can be certain that their seed has been fully tested according to EU regulations, that it contains no untested strains, and that it will be genetically uniform.

Information about what's in the seed packet, such as the number of plants it's likely to yield, is invaluable for gardeners. Unfortunately it's not required by law. The same applies to the sell-by date after which germination cannot be guaranteed. You can work out the year in which the seed was packed by looking at the packet, but it's hardly significant. Seeds are a natural product, and those of different species and varieties will have widely varying life-spans. For instance, parsnip, chive, aster or parsley seeds will quickly lose their ability to germinate, while others will remain viable for several years as long as you store them under suitable conditions.

For this reason good seed manufacturers sell their products in hermetically sealed packages. This stops premature ageing of the seeds as a result of high air humidity. Once these packages are opened, the seed should be used in the normal way, generally within one or two years.

Unsold seed is stored in screw-top jars. It's important to ensure that the air inside is dry when the seed packets are put in, since humidity will quickly spoil the seed. In the winter, well before new seed is required, the manufacturers carry out a germination test to see which seed packets have to be discarded.

This is done in the laboratory, in conditions similar to the normal germinating environment — daytime temperatures of 86°F (30°C) and night temperatures of 68°F (20°C) are suitable for 90 per cent of all plant species. The seed is laid on moistened fleece on trays, in Petri dishes or (with leguminous plants, for instance) in sand. It's then kept on a germinating bench or in a germinating cupboard. However, this test only demonstrates the results under optimum conditions, and in practice seedlings will be vulnerable to pests, wind and unfavourable temperatures. For this reason further tests are carried out in soil cultures to see how the seed behaves in more stressful surroundings.

Commercial seed is usually tested at least three times before it comes onto the market, so it's normally of high quality. What's more, it's produced in more favourable climatic conditions than those of wet and windy Britain. Most of it comes from sunnier regions with milder winters, such as California, Australia, Italy or southern France.

Testing seed quality in a laboratory.

Too wet, too dry, too warm — if you want to sow successfully, you should always read the instructions on the packet.

Home germination tests

Some simple germination tests can be done at home just as effectively as in the laboratory.

The paper method is very effective with fine flower or vegetable seeds. Lay some fleece, some blotting paper or some paper handkerchiefs across a cereal bowl. Moisten it without letting any water stand on the surface. Count out a good round number of seeds (say, 50 or 100), and spread them out over the paper. Stretch some clingfilm over the bowl or put it in a

plastic bag. Leave it somewhere that is well lit but not sunny, and keep it at the plant's optimum germination temperature. After a few days, count how many seeds have germinated.

If you achieve a success rate of around 75 per cent, then the seed is perfectly usable. If it's between 50 and 75 per cent, you'll have to sow more densely. But if fewer than half the seeds germinate, then you'll be better off buying new seed. The only exceptions to this rule are herbs, which are invariably poor germinators.

Bean and pea seeds need plenty of air to germinate; when sown in the garden they can't cope with deep sowing or waterlogged soil. They react

better to the germination test if they're sown in a well-ventilated medium such as sand. Fill the bowl with sand and wet it so that it's moderately damp — not like mud! Press the seeds in, and place a second bowl like a lid over the top. Keep it at around 64–68°F (18–20°C), and the results will be visible after just one week.

With some hard-shelled seeds, like those of palm, coffee or bananas, it's a good idea to pre-soak them for a day in luke-warm water. Then you can sow them in the normal way. The same goes for seeds that lie in the soil for a long time, like parsnips or parsley: they'll germinate much faster if they've been soaked for a day before sowing. The procedure is quite simple: put the seeds in a linen bag, soak the bag, and after a day, sow the seed straight from the bag. In the summer this method is also helpful for lettuce seeds, which often germinate poorly at temperatures above 64°F (18°C). Wet the seeds and put them in the linen bag, put the bag away in the fridge, and plant the seeds straight from the fridge the following evening

Most vegetable seeds will germinate readily without any special treatment. Chitting (or chipping) is a technique to help nature on its way with hard-coated seeds like cucumbers and melons, and also with sweet peas. Just nick the seeds with a knife or a file after they've been soaked.

Germinate the seeds on moist blotting paper, and sow them individually in small pots. Sow flat seeds on edge, so as to avoid rot. Very fine seed should be mixed with dry silver sand before sowing.

Dressing the seed kills any fungi that may have become attached to them. Nowadays most commercial seed remains untreated, and is left in its natural state. If the seed *has* been treated, then the packet must say so, although fewer seed dressings are allowed these days.

The best way to protect your plants from biting, stinging or devouring insects is to cover them up with a material such as garden fleece.

Sowing indoors

We have already talked about the advantages of good preparation, and also about containers and seed compost.

If you have enough space on a window-sill or in your greenhouse, there's nothing simpler than sowing seeds in 3.5-5-in (9-13-cm) plastic half-trays or pots. Large seeds can be sown in the individual cells of cellular trays, or in peat pots filled with compost, or else in peat pellets (Jiffy 7s).

Fill the container with compost and firm it down gently with a piece of board. Use the base of another pot to level the surface of the compost, which needs to be approximately ½ in (1 cm) below the rim of the container.

Now you can sprinkle the surface with water using a fine-rose watering can, and leave it to drain before sowing; the idea is to have the soil moist, but not wet, when you come to scatter the seeds over the surface. It's also quite a good idea to sow your larger seeds in rows.

Most seeds will need to be covered after sowing. Spread them thinly over the compost, either by sprinkling pinches from your finger and thumb, or by tapping them carefully out of the seed packet. Avoid oversowing, as a mass of weak seedlings will be prone to various fungal diseases.

Now cover the seeds by sifting a little compost over them.

As a general rule, you should try to cover your seeds with their own depth of compost or silver sand.

Don't cover very fine seed (such as begonia, lobelia or petunia) with the compost. These seeds are very small indeed, and the best way to deal with them is to mix them with a small amount of fine silver sand, then shake the mixture evenly over the compost, in a thin layer, and leave it uncovered.

Finally, it's a good idea to label each pot or tray. Always include the name of the variety — and perhaps the date of sowing as well.

Most (though not all) seeds will need darkness in order to germinate successfully, so cover the pots and trays with

When you're propagating from seed on a window-sill, sow the seeds thinly, press them down firmly, and finally cover them up nicely.

paper, then put a sheet of glass on top. Leave them at a fairly warm temperature (64–70°F; 18–21°C); ideally they should be in a thermostatically controlled propagator or greenhouse, or on the window-sill of a centrally heated room that is kept at the correct temperature all the time.

Check every day for signs of germination. The paper should absorb any condensation and stop it dripping onto the soil: if it seems to be getting saturated, you should change it. As soon as the seedlings start to appear above the soil, take the paper away and prop up the sheet of glass. It's true that seedlings need some ventilation and light, but don't expose them to direct sunlight or you'll risk scorching them.

Pots on a window-sill should be turned every couple of days: this will stop the seedlings becoming leggy. If you're growing them in a propagator, then make sure that you open the vents.

Don't let the compost dry out at this stage: mist the emerging seedlings with a fine sprayer, or use a watering can with a fine rose. Lettuce, kohlrabi and many flowers need to be placed in a brighter position that is also cooler (by about 7–9F°; 4–5C°). Otherwise the seedlings will grow too long and too soft — and only small, squat seedlings are easy to prick out.

You'll need to prick out these young plants to give them enough space to grow and develop. Fill your pots or trays with some lightly fertilised potting compost.

To release the seedlings from the seed compost, use one of those specially shaped plastic widgers (available in a gardening shop or centre). Hold the seedling by its seed leaves, and use the widger to ease it out gently so the roots remain undamaged.

Now make an appropriately sized hole in the potting compost, and put the seedling into it with its roots hanging straight down; don't let them get twisted. If the roots are long, shorten them slightly to encourage side growth — that way they'll form a root ball.

When you've finished, the seedling with its seed leaves should protrude approximately ½–1 in (1–2 cm) above the soil surface — if it's too deep it may rot, and if it's too shallow it can easily fall over.

Prick the soil all around, and push some of it in towards the plant to give it more grip. Finally, moisten the compost thoroughly with a fine-rose watering can, and put the container in a well-lit position where there's plenty of humidity in the air.

If the soil is very loamy, then bank up the soil before sowing, and fill the drill afterwards with crumbly, well-rotted garden compost.

Sowing outdoors

Direct sowing outdoors is suitable for beans, peas, spinach, carrots and herbs, and also for fast-growing flower seeds like those of the sweet pea (*Lathyrus*), *Lavatera*, marigold or *Cosmea*. From the end of March on you can sow them straight into shallow seed drills without any difficulty.

However, if these plants are going to grow in the way you want, you must be sure to prepare the seedbed in the right way before you start. Dig the soil in autumn and winter,

then leave it to settle so that the structure forms a pattern of tiny vertical holes (known as **capillary pores**). Moisture is then sucked up through these holes towards the surface to replace what is lost through evaporation. If you turn over the soil — by digging or hoeing, for instance — this capillary action is interrupted and the moisture is trapped below the surface.

To make sure that the new seedlings can benefit from capillary action, don't use anything except a rake or a cultivator to loosen the surface. If possible, don't go any deeper than the depth of a seed drill — that's about 1 in (2-3 cm), or 1-2 in (3-5 cm) if we're talking about peas and beans.

There are risks involved in raking the soil any deeper: you could leave your seeds lying in loose earth without any access to the moisture contained in the soil.

Now everything depends on plenty of rain, or a regular soaking from a watering can. This is particularly important in the case of seed tapes or pelleted seeds: these need constant, even humidity and the number of seeds has been deliberately reduced.

Rake the surface of the soil to create a fine texture. If necessary, you can rake in a 1-2-in (3-5-cm) layer of well-rotted garden compost or a small amount of fertiliser beforehand. It's best to use an organic fertiliser that takes a long time to break down, or a slow-release fertiliser that provides nutrients at a very slow rate. This is because freshly sown seed generally needs very few nutrients at first. Later on, when the larger leaves have formed, it will need more.

Use a taut garden line to mark out the edges of paths between the beds, then mark them more definitely with the handle or the flat of your rake. Now stamp the paths down with your feet to make them firm.

If you have very heavy soil that's liable to become caked, it's a good idea to lay down planks for walking on. That way you'll keep your shoes cleaner, as well.

For a short person the ideal width for a seedbed is 40 in

100 cm), with the rows 10 in 25 cm) apart. However, a width of 4 ft (120 cm) is better if you're tall. You can use a row marker to give you the right distance between rows: 0 in (25 cm) for lettuces and carrots; 16-20 in (40-50 cm) or cabbages; and 4-6 in (10-15 m) for radishes, cress and looseleaf lettuce.

For each row, make a drill of he appropriate depth — some-where between about ½ in and 2 in (1-5 cm). Drills can be drawn with the edge of a draw hoe against a straight, taut

A row marker is an extremely useful piece of equipment.

garden line. For shorter rows, you can simply press the handle of your rake into the soil. Be careful not to make the drill too deep, and keep it the same depth all the way along. If you sow this way, you'll be able to tell the difference between the crop and any weed seedlings that appear.

> Most small veget-able seeds don't need to be covered by more than ½-¾ in (1-2 cm) of soil. Larger seeds such as peas and beans shouldn't be sown any deeper than 2 in (5 cm).

You can sow as soon as the soil surface is sufficiently dry and crumbly (in other words, when it isn't sticky any more). Just take a small sample and test it by rubbing it between your fingers.

With a little practice you'll soon be able to sow the seeds thinly and at regular intervals along the drills. Make a crease in one side of the open seed packet, tap it gently with your index finger and the seeds will trickle out a few at a time. The more thinly and evenly you distribute them, the better the result will be, as the seedlings will have plenty of time to grow before they start to crowd each other.

Sowing aids

You can buy a variety of sowing aids that will help you to sow thinly and evenly without too much skill and effort.

In the case of **pelleted seeds**, the individual seeds have been coated in a layer of clay to make them larger and easier to handle.

Seed tapes consist of paper tape with individual seeds stuck to it at regular intervals.

So-called **seed sticks** are match-shaped seed carriers made of strong cardboard. They make it easier to sow fine seeds out in the garden, and easier still to sow them indoors, in pots. Each stick is marked to show the proper sowing depth for the seeds.

With seed tapes and pelleted seeds it's often helpful to water them as soon as you've put them in the open drills, just to make sure they're properly

Carrots must always be sown individually.

Each of these pellets contains just a single seed.

bedded in. Only then should you rake some loose soil across to cover them to the right depth. This should be between about ½ in and 1 in (1–3 cm) depending on the species. Don' forget to give the whole lot a thorough watering after that, using a fine-rose watering can.

If you have problems sowing fine seeds such as carrots, parsley, *Clarkia* or *Lavatera* (to name but a few), mix the seed with sharp sand so it's easier to spread it more thinly.

If you're sowing a flower meadow or a lawn, then you may find it helpful to replace the sharp sand with vermiculite This is a naturally occurring clay mineral that's light in weight

---

If your soil tends to become muddy or contains a lot of clay, cover it with well-rotted garden compost, seed compost or bark compost, and work this in thoroughly to lighten the soil before you start to sow.

---

and light in colour. The advantage of it is that you can see where your seeds have fallen and how densely they've been sown. If the seed is sown too densely, it will germinate in clumps, and you'll need to thin out the seedlings as soon as they're big enough for you to get a grip on them; otherwise they can't be expected to grow very well.

Radishes appear quickly after sowing, making them the ideal marker crop.

Carrots must be sown at intervals of 1-2½ in (3-6 cm), radishes 2-3 in (5-8 cm) apart, and cabbages between 16 in (40 cm) and 24 in (60 cm) apart depending on the variety.

Carrots, parsley, parsnips, scorzonera and various herbs take several weeks to sprout, which means that at first you can't see the rows, and can't therefore hoe in between them to remove weeds. The trick is to sow a few quick-germinating **marker seeds** such as radishes or looseleaf lettuce (spring onions are good for this, too). That way you can see where the rows are, and you can also enjoy an early harvest!

Careful watering is essential in the early stages. When you've filled in the seed drills, water them again with a fine-rose watering can. If the soil is sandy, use more water; if it's liable to turn to mud, water more carefully. Don't allow a crust to form on the surface, as this will stop the new plants emerging; if necessary, use a hand cultivator to loosen up the surface.

It goes almost without saying that you should never let the seedbed dry out: keep it moist right up until the time for planting on. Often this isn't easy, as the surface dries out quickly in hot weather. Always water in the evening, when the moisture will be properly absorbed — never in the heat of the day — and always water thoroughly, so the moisture really gets down into the soil.

Take plenty of time over watering. If you use a garden spray, leave it on for several hours. However, if you use a watering can, it's easier to control where the water goes. Continuous superficial watering can often cause damage in the long run; in time the deeper roots, deprived of water, will begin to die off.

Protecting seeds:
Fleece (or plastic sheeting with slits or holes) keeps the air humid for a long time, and stops your seedlings drying out. It also protects your seeds from birds. They love eating the germinating seeds, and when they realise they're onto a good thing they'll come back to feast on your seedlings. Another way to keep the birds off is to use polythene or wire netting, or crossed-over lengths of wire.

Vegetables

Crop rotation, intercropping and companion planting

There are some questions that gardeners face every year. What will grow in this tiny garden? Where will my vegetables and flowers do best? How can I avoid taking all the goodness out of the soil? Do my vegetable beds always have to lie empty for part of the year?

You can solve the last of these problems by **intercropping** — planting fast-growing crops and slower-growing crops together in the same bed. **Crop rotation** is one way to deal with some of the others.

What we're describing here is a three-year rotation plan, but it's just one example of many possible plans. Once you've set it up, you'll only need to change things round once a year. Each crop is moved to a different bed every year until, in the fourth year, it returns to its original bed. Some intercropping is also possible within individual beds.

Like the traditional country practice of fertilising with animal manure, part of the art of crop rotation is to plan for the different amounts of nutrients that the various crops take out of the soil. The principle applies especially to light or sandy soils, where soil nutrients are quickly lost. It also helps prevent the build-up of diseases and pests specific to particular crops.

Divide your plot into three beds, with a fourth set aside for permanent crops like rhubarb and asparagus. Then divide the crops into three groups: brassicas (cabbages and their close relatives, including some root vegetables like turnips); roots (potatoes, parsnips, carrots etc.); and pulses (peas and beans) together with onions and salad crops. In year one plant brassicas in bed one, roots in bed two and pulses etc. in bed three. In year two put roots in bed one, pulses etc. in bed two, and brassicas in bed three. In the third year pulses etc. go in bed one, brassicas in bed two, and roots in bed three. Start the cycle again in the fourth year.

If you rotate your crops so that each bed is occupied by members of a different botanical family every year, you'll avoid passing on pests and diseases that attack specific groups of plants. For example, clubroot affects all members of the cabbage family (Cruciferae), which includes wallflowers and stocks as well as cabbages, radishes and kohlrabi. Carrots, celery and parsley all belong to the Umbelliferae, making them all potential hosts for the same nematode worm. Strawberries, roses and apple trees are all Rosaceae, so they're all affected by specific pests and diseases common to that family. Clearly it's sound gardening practice not to replant an area with a species from the same family.

If you plant the same crop in the same bed two years running it keeps taking the same nutrients out of the soil; it also keeps putting the same substances *into* the soil, which can damage later crops. Very few plants will thrive if they're sown in the same place every year. Rotation ensures that at least two years elapse before a crop is repeated.

Some plants, however, will improve the soil and boost the growth of other plants. The roots of peas and beans, for example, leave nitrogen behind them that can be used by the brassica crop that follows them in the rotation cycle.

Obviously your choice of crops will depend on personal taste, but if space is limited go for high-yield species — runner beans rather than French beans, and spinach beet rather than spinach. Courgettes, onions and carrots all produce good returns for the space they occupy.

To get maximum use of your growing space, try intercropping with catch and succession crops. **Catch crops** are quick-growing vegetables sown early before a main crop is planted out: salad onions, for example, can be sown on the brassica plot in March before the winter cabbage is planted out in July. Catch crops can also be grown between slower-growing vegetables, then lifted to give the slower ones more space — for instance, you can plant radishes or lettuces between rows of peas. **Succession crops**, on the other hand, are quick-maturing species planted after a main crop has been cleared.

Some plants grow better when planted alongside others from a particular group or species — a phenomenon that is exploited in **companion planting**. A good

There are various plants that protect their neighbours from nematode damage. They include some beautiful and very effective summer flowers such as coneflower (*Rudbeckia*), tickseed (*Coreopsis*), blanket flower (*Gaillardia*) and the two marigold genera: *Calendula* and especially *Tagetes*. All of them have an important 'medicinal' role in mixed cultivation. Sow them over whole areas like green manures, and leave them to grow for about 100–120 days (approximately 4 months). Finally dig them in.

example of this is growing onions next to rows of carrots: the smell of the onions seems to deter carrot flies. Garlic, lavender, sage, leeks and chives are all said to repel insects, while marigolds are supposed to keep whitefly away from vegetables and flowers. Not all plants make good companions. Some would simply deprive each other of nutrients, and others smother their neighbours, while closely related species such as potatoes and tomatoes are vulnerable to the same diseases.

All these points must be taken into consideration when planning your vegetable beds and your crop-rotation cycles.

Mixed cultivation in a traditional cottage garden.

29

Seed table and growing instructions for vegetables

Vegetables	germination period days	germination temperature °F (°C)	distance between rows in (cm)	sowing time	where?
artichokes	15-25	64-77 (18-25)	30 (80)	Feb./May	gr
French beans	7-15	59-77 (15-25)	12 (30)	May/Jul.	sd
runner beans	10-20	64-77 (18-25)	30 (80)	mid-May	sd
peas	7-15	50-68 (10-20)	8-12 (20-30)	early Apr.	sd
corn salad	25-35	50-72 (10-22)	4-6 (10-15)	Aug.-Oct.	sd
bulb fennel	15-25	61-72 (16-22)	12-16 (30-40)	Jun./Jul.	sd
cucumbers (outdoor)	6-15	64-77 (18-25)	40 (100)	mid-May	sd ft
cucumbers (greenh.)	6-15	72-82 (22-28)	40 (100)	Feb.-May	gr
cauliflowers	5-15	64-72 (18-22)	20 (50)	Feb.-May	gf sd ft
broccoli	5-15	64-72 (18-22)	16-20 (40-50)	Apr.-May	gf sd ft
Chinese cabbage	5-15	64-72 (18-22)	12-16 (30-40)	Jul./Aug.	sd
sprouts	6-15	64-72 (18-22)	24 (60)	Apr.	sd
red/white cabbage	8-16	59-72 (15-22)	20 (50)	Jan./May	sd
kohlrabi	5-15	59-72 (15-22)	12 (30)	Apr./Jun.	gf sd ft
Swiss chard	10-20	59-72 (15-22)	12 (30)	Mar.-Oct.	sd ft gr
melons	8-20	72-79 (22-26)	40 (100)	Apr.-May	gr ft
carrots	14-28	50-72 (10-22)	12 (30)	Mar./Jun.	sd
leeks	14-25	64-68 (18-20)	16-20 (40-50)	Mar./Apr.	sd
onions	14-30	59-64 (15-18)	12 (30)	Mar.-Apr.	sd
radishes	6-14	54-68 (12-20)	8 (20)	Jan./Aug.	sd gf gr ft
beetroot	10-20	59-72 (15-22)	10 (25)	Apr./Jun.	sd
cabbage lettuce	10-15	46-61 (8-16)	12 (30)	Mar./Jul. (sd Oct./Feb.)	sd ft gf gr
chicory	8-15	61-72 (16-22)	16 (40)	Apr./May	sd
endives	8-15	64-77 (18-25)	12-16 (30-40)	Jun.-Jul.	sd
radicchio	10-16	61-68 (16-20)	2 (5)	May-Jun.	sd
celery	18-30	64-72 (18-22)	12 (30)	Feb.-Mar.	sd
celeriac	18-30	64-72 (18-22)	16 (40)	Mar.	gr gf
spinach	8-20	5-20 (41-68)	8 (20)	Mar./May	sd ft
tomatoes	8-20	64-77 (18-25)	48 (80)	early Mar.	gr
sweet peppers	10-20	68-77 (20-25)	24 (60)	Feb./Mar.	gr
courgettes, pumpkins	6-15	64-77 (18-25)	48 (80)	Apr./May	gr sd

eed table for medicinal and culinary herbs

Herbs	sowing months	where?	germination temperature °F (°C)	germination period days	seed viability years
basil	May-Jun.	gf gr	61-77 (16-25)	14-25	4-5
borage	Apr.-Jun.		59-77 (15-25)	21-35	2-3
salad burnet	Apr.-Jun.		59-77 (15-25)	20-30	2-3
caraway	Mar.-Jun.		61-72 (16-22)	20-35	3-4
chamomile	Apr.-May		61-72 (16-22)	15-30	2-3
chervil	Apr.-Aug.		61-77 (16-25)	20-30	3-4
Chinese chives	Apr.-Aug.		64-77 (18-25)	20-35	2-3
chives	Apr.-Aug.		59-72 (15-22)	20-30	1-3
coriander	Apr.-Jun.		61-77 (16-25)	20-30	2-3
watercress	Mar.-Aug.		43-57 (6-14)	12-25	4-5
dandelion	Mar.-Aug.	sd	54-64 (12-18)	10-30	1-3
dill	Apr.-Aug.		59-68 (15-20)	20-35	2-3
fennel	Apr.-Jun.	sd	61-72 (16-22)	15-25	2-3
lavender	Apr.-Jun.	gr sd	64-77 (18-25)	20-30	2-3
lemon balm	Apr.-May	gf gr sd	68-86 (20-30)	20-40	2-3
lovage	Apr.-Jun.	gf gr	64-77 (18-25)	20-30	1-2
sweet marjoram	Apr.-Jun.		59-77 (15-25)	21-35	2-3
milk thistle	May-Jun.		59-77 (15-25)	20-30	3-4
oregano	Apr.-May	gf gr sd	68-86 (20-30)	30-45	1-3
parsley	Mar.-Aug.		59-77 (15-25)	15-30	2
peppermint	Mar.-May	gf sd	68-77 (20-25)	20-35	2-3
summer purslane	Apr.-Jun.		64-77 (18-25)	6-15	3-4
winter purslane	Aug.-May		under 59 (15)	8-14	2-3
rosemary	Mar.-Jun.	gf gr	68-82 (20-28)	14-35	2-3
sage	Mar.-Jun.	gf gr sd	68-77 (20-25)	20-35	2-3
savory	Apr.-Jun.		61-77 (16-25)	18-28	2-3
sorrel	Apr.-Aug.		59-72 (15-22)	10-20	4-5
tarragon	Mar.-May	gf sd	64-77 (18-25)	10-30	2-3
thyme	Mar.-May	gf gr sd	68-79 (20-26)	30-45	2-3
valerian	Apr.-May	sd gf	50-68 (10-20)	20-30	2-3

ft = under film/tunnel; **sd** = sow direct; **gf** = garden frame; **gr** = greenhouse

Flowers for the garden

Propagating summer flowers from seed

Most flowers will bloom during the warmer part of the year. Even so, the term 'summer flowers' is normally used to describe those easy-to-grow flowers that can be used to fill your beds, patios, containers and borders with a sea of bright colours for just a few months of the year.

Any specialist gardening shop or gardening centre should be able to offer you seeds for hundreds of different species and varieties of flower, which makes for thousands of different combinations. However, the flowers that are most commonly available are generally those that are nicest to look at and easiest to look after.

Begonias, petunias, flowering tobacco (*Nicotiana*), floss flower (*Ageratum*), *Lobelia erinus*, snapdragon (*Antirrhinum majus*), *Penstemon barbatus*, and busy Lizzie (*Impatiens*) grow from very fine seed, which should be sown in February and pricked out twice after that until the first flowers appear in May.

March is the time for sowing most of the reasonably hardy flowers — marigolds (*Tagetes*), *Celosia argentea*, spider flower (*Cleome spinosa*), cathedral bells (*Cobaea scandens*), *Alyssum benthami*, castor-oil plant (*Ricinus*) and zinnias. These can be propagated from seed in much the same way as vegetables — on a window-sill, or in a greenhouse or garden frame.

Many summer flowers can be sown straight out in the garden,

Summer flowers shouldn't be grown just to fill gaps.

including clarkias, chrysanthemums, toadflax (*Linaria*) and
Centaurea (for cut flowers).
You can sow them thinly into
shallow seed drills ½-1 in (1-3
cm) deep, thinning out later if
seedlings have grown too close
together. You could also sow
them in a garden frame, or in a

carefully prepared seedbed with
fine, crumbly soil. However, you
may need to cover the seedbed
with fleece or perforated plastic
film to stop it drying out, and
also to protect the young plants
from birds.

From April onwards you can
use a similar seedbed protected

in the same way to grow more
tender plants with fine seeds.
Asters, *Lavatera*, marigolds
(*Calendula*), and also summer-
flowering *Cheiranthus*, pansies
and forget-me-nots, grow well in
such a bed if they're sown in
rows 4-6 in (10-15 cm) apart.
Use a suitably humus-rich seeding compost or finely sieved,
well-rotted garden compost to
get the best results. As soon as
the seedlings are big enough to
get a grip on, transplant them
into the bed where you mean to
display them.

From May on you can start
sowing biennial flowers like
Canterbury bells, foxgloves,
Iceland poppies, sweet William,
forget-me-nots, daisies and
pansies. To germinate properly
pansies and daisies in particular
need plenty of oxygen, moisture
and shade, and relatively cool
temperatures of 59-63°F
(15-17°C). In a hot summer
these conditions may be difficult to achieve without some
temporary shading. Lay some
rough, wet sacking over the
seedbeds and keep it moist all
the time. The heat absorbed by
the water as it evaporates will
keep the seedbeds cooler. Sow
the seeds very shallowly, covering them with no more than
¼ in (5 mm) of soil. Pansy seeds
are covered with a thin oily film;
put a little damp sand in your
hand, and rub the film away.
The seeds will only take a few
days to germinate. Remove the
sacking as soon as soon as the
seedlings appear, so that they
don't get caught in it.

SEED PROPAGATION

Seed table for annuals

Plant	sowing months	where?	germination temperature °F (°C)	germination period days	seed viability years
Acroclinum syn. *Helipterum*	4-5	sd	59-68 (15-20)	15-25	3
Ageratum (floss flower)	2-3	gr	72-79 (22-26)	10-20	2-3
Alyssum (sweet alyssum)	3-4	gr	64-72 (18-22)	6-10	2-3
Amaranthus	4-5	sd	64-72 (18-22)	7-14	4-5
Anchusa	3-4	sd	64-75 (18-24)	10-20	2-3
Antirrhinum (snapdragon)	2-3	gr	50-68 (10-20)	20-30	2-3
Arctotis (African daisy)	3-4	gr	68-79 (20-26)	20-30	2-3
Begonia	12-2	gr	64-77 (18-25)	15-25	2-3
Brachycome	3-5	gr sd	64-72 (18-22)	14-20	2-3
Calendula (pot marigold)	3-8	sd gr	50-68 (10-20)	8-15	3-4
Callistephus (China aster)	3-5	sd gf	64-70 (18-21)	8-20	1-2
Celosia (cockscomb)	3-4	gr	64-72 (18-22)	14-20	2-3
Centaurea (cornflower)	3-9	sd	50-68 (10-20)	14-20	3-4
Chrysanthemum (annual chrysanthemum)	4-6	sd	50-68 (10-20)	14-20	3-5
Clarkia	4-5	sd	59-72 (15-22)	10-16	2-3
Cleome (spider flower)	2-3	gr	64-77 (18-25)	18-30	2-3
Cobaea (cathedral bells)	2-3	gr	64-77 (18-25)	15-25	2-3
Coleus (flame nettle)	2-3	gr	64-77 (18-25)	15-20	2-3
Convolvulus	3-4	gr	64-77 (18-25)	8-15	3-4
Cosmos bipinnatus (cosmea)	4-5	sd gf	59-77 (15-25)	12-20	3-4
Cosmos sulphureus	3-5	gr gf	64-77 (18-25)	12-25	3-4
Cuphea (cigar plant)	2-3	gr	64-77 (18-25)	15-25	2-3
Delphinium (annual delphinium)	2-4	sd	54-61 (12-16)	12-20	2-3
Dimorphotheca (Cape marigold)	4-5	sd	59-77 (15-25)	10-18	3-5
Eschscholtzia (Californian poppy)	3-9	sd	50-72 (10-22)	8-15	3-4

months 1–12 = January-December; **sd** = sow direct; **gf** = garden frame; **gr** = greenhouse

Seed table for annuals (continued)

Plant	sowing months	where?	germination temperature °F (°C)	germination period days	seed viability years
Euphorbia marginata (snow-in-summer)	4-5	sd	59-77 (15-25)	8-15	3-4
Eustoma	2-3	gr	64-72 (18-22)	20-30	2-3
Gazania	2-4	gr	64-77 (18-25)	10-25	1-3
Gilia, Ipomopsis	4-5	sd	64-77 (18-25)	18-25	2-3
Godetia	4-5	sd	59-68 (15-20)	10-20	3-4
Gomphrena (globe amaranth)	4-5	sd gf	59-72 (15-22)	10-20	3-4
Briza (quaking grass)	3-5	sd	64-77 (18-25)	10-25	2-3
Coix (Job's tears)	3-4	sd gf	68-77 (20-25)	10-25	2-3
Hordeum (foxtail barley)	3-5	sd	64-77 (18-25)	10-25	2-3
Lagurus (hare's tail grass)	3-5	sd	64-77 (18-25)	15-25	2-3
Gypsophila (baby's breath)	4-5	sd	59-68 (15-20)	15-25	2-3
Helianthus (sunflower)	4-5	sd	59-77 (15-25)	10-20	3-5
Helichrysum	4-5	sd	59-77 (15-25)	15-25	2-4
Iberis (candytuft)	4-6	sd	50-68 (10-20)	8-20	2-3
Impatiens (busy Lizzie)	2-3	gr	64-77 (18-25)	18-30	2-3
Ipomoea (morning glory)	3-4	gr	64-77 (18-25)	8-20	2-3
Kochia (burning bush)	4-5	sd	59-72 (15-22)	10-20	2-3
Lathyrus	3-5	sd	50-64 (10-18)	10-20	3-4
Lavatera	3-6	gf sd	64-77 (18-25)	10-20	3-4
Limnanthes (poached-egg plant)	3-5, 9	gf sd	64-77 (18-25)	14-20	3-4
Linaria (toadflax)	4-5	sd	59-77 (15-25)	8-20	3-4
Lobelia	2-3	gr	64-77 (18-25)	5-15	2-3
Matthiola (stock)	2-9	sd gf	59-72 (15-22)	8-20	3-5
Matricaria (feverfew)	3-5	gf gr	59-68 (15-20)	10-20	3-4
Mesembryanthemum	3-5	sd gr	59-77 (15-25)	8-20	2-3
Mimulus (monkey musk)	2-5	gr	54-64 (12-18)	10-20	2-3
Nemesia	2-6	sd gr	64-77 (18-25)	10-20	2-3
Nemophila (baby blue-eyes)	4-6	sd	59-77 (15-25)	10-20	3-4

Seed table for annuals (continued)

Plant	sowing months	where?	germination temperature °F (°C)	germination period days	seed viability years
Nicotiana (flowering tobacco)	3-4	gr	64-77 (18-25)	15-25	2-3
Nigella (love-in-a-mist)	4-8	sd	59-72 (15-22)	10-20	2-3
Papaver (poppy)	3-10	sd	50-64 (10-18)	15-25	3-4
Penstemon	2-3	gr	64-72 (18-22)	15-30	2-3
Perilla	2-3	gr	68-79 (20-26)	12-20	2-3
Petunia	2-3	gr	64-72 (18-22)	10-20	2-3
Phacelia tanacetifolia	5-8	sd	59-68 (15-20)	8-15	3-4
Phacelia campanularia (California bluebell)	6-7	sd	59-68 (15-20)	8-15	2-3
Phlox drummondii (annual phlox)	3-5	sd	64-77 (18-25)	15-25	2-3
Portulaca	3-6	sd	59-72 (15-22)	8-15	2-3
Reseda (mignonette)	4-6	sd	64-77 (18-25)	10-20	3-4
Ricinus (castor-oil plant)	3-4	gr	64-77 (18-25)	12-25	3-5
Rudbeckia (coneflower)	4-5	sd	59-68 (15-20)	15-25	3-4
Salpiglossis (painted tongue)	3-5	sd gr	64-77 (18-25)	15-25	2-3
Salvia (sage)	2-3	gr	68-77 (20-25)	8-25	2-3
Sanvitalia (creeping zinnia)	3-4	gr	64-72 (18-22)	8-18	3-4
Scabiosa (scabious)	4-6	sd	59-72 (15-22)	10-20	2-3
Schizanthus (butterfly flower)	4-9	sd gr	59-72 (15-22)	10-20	3-4
Silene (campion)	4-5	sd	50-68 (10-20)	12-20	3-4
Limonium (sea lavender)	4-5	sd	64-72 (18-22)	12-25	3-4
Tagetes (marigold)	2-5	gr sd	64-77 (18-25)	8-20	2-3
Thunbergia	3-4	gr	64-77 (18-25)	15-25	2-3
Tropaeolum (nasturtium)	3-5	sd	64-72 (18-22)	10-20	3-4
Verbena (vervain)	2-3	gr	64-72 (18-22)	15-32	2-3
Zea (ornamental maize)	4-5	gr sd	64-77 (18-25)	8-20	3-4
Zinnia	3-5	gf sd	68-77 (20-25)	8-20	2-3

months 1–12 = January–December; **sd** = sow direct; **gf** = garden frame; **gr** = greenhouse

Seed table for biennials

Pansies germinate better under damp sacking.

Plant species	sowing months	germination period temp. °F (°C)	days	viab. yrs
Alcea rosea (hollyhock)	6-8	59-72 (15-22)	5-12	3-4
Bellis (biennial daisy)	6-8	64-72 (18-22)	18-20	2-3
Campanula medium (Canterbury bell)	6-7	54-72 (12-22)	12-25	3-4
Cheiranthus cheiri (wallflower)	6-7	50-68 (10-20)	8-15	3-4
Dianthus barbatus (sweet William)	6-8	59-68 (15-20)	10-20	3-4
Digitalis purpurea (foxglove)	7-8	64-72 (18-22)	15-25	3-4
Lunaria biennis (honesty)	5-7	54-68 (12-20)	8-15	3-4
Myosotis (forget-me-not)	7-8	59-72 (15-22)	8-15	3-4
Papaver nudicaule (Iceland poppy)	7-8	64-72 (18-22)	10-20	3-4
Viola × wittrockiana (garden pansy)	6-8	59-64 (15-18)	8-15	2-3

Wild flowers and flower meadows

Sowing in rows isn't suitable for wild flowers, flower meadows or the combinations of herbs and summer flowers that you might find in a cottage garden. Like a lawn, they'll grow much better if you sow them **broadcast**, scattering them thinly all over the bed. Rake them gently into the soil, and keep the bed moist all the time.

If you want to make a lawn look natural without transforming the whole surface, then one possible alternative is to create **island beds** of flowers. Make a series of circular or kidney-shaped seedbeds in suitable locations, and sow them with any wild annuals or perennials you like (you'll find that there's a massive choice). You can create a new display of wild flowers every year, and if you want you can spread the seeds outside the confines of the bed so the flowers gradually merge with the lawn.

A **flower meadow** will look most appropriate in a country garden, or next to a water garden complete with a pond, a stream and a marshy area. Make sure your meadow is large enough for people to enjoy it.

Loam, clay or nutrient-rich soils aren't very suitable — the grass and clover species will spread too vigorously after a few years, and eventually they'll choke the wild flowers. Strange as it may seem, poor-quality, unfertilised, sandy soils are actually much better.

If you have a flower meadow, remember to mow it once or twice a year, and always keep to the paths. Even dogs and cats can make a mess of the hordes of graceful but delicate flowers.

If you're looking for a half-way house, then one possible option is to combine a more formal lawn next to the house with a flower meadow towards the edge of your garden — that way both artifice and nature can have their say.

One alternative for a smaller garden is to plant a lawn with **wild flowers** that have more rosette-like leaves. Daisies, primroses, speedwell and violets aren't disturbed by mowing because their leaves lie so close to the ground, and they can happily survive being trodden on by clumsy adults or active children. Crocuses, snowdrops, glory-of-the-snow (*Chionodoxa*) and autumn crocus (*Colchicum autumnale*) will also do very well here, just so long as you hold off mowing in the early spring until they have drawn in their leaves.

How do you produce a flower meadow? It's useless just throwing seed in among the grass, because the seeds have to be in full contact with the soil in order to germinate.

Scarifying the lawn is also ineffective: it simply encourages the grass, which then competes even more strongly with the

Fields of wild flowers are a paradise for butterflies and bees.

Flower meadows are simply a joy to look at.

flowers. Some people even suggest that you should wait for the soil to become exhausted and then allow the flowers to seed naturally from the surrounding area. However, this approach calls for a great deal of patience!

It's possible to run a cultivator through an existing lawn and then sow it with wild flowers. But the most effective method is to start the meadow completely from scratch.

The best times to sow are in the spring from late March to May, or in the autumn between August and October.

It's vital to prepare the soil properly beforehand: this will save a lot of extra work in the long run. Use crumbly loam, peat or layers of well-structured, weed-free humus to create the varied conditions that the wild flowers need.

Buy a seed mixture that contains plenty of different species which have all been propagated in conditions that correspond to your own local climate. The first flowers to reveal their glories will be the fast-growing farmland species such as corn poppy, wild chrysanthemums, corn cockle and cornflower. As in natural situations, the open soil is quickly colonised by a host of

longer-lasting wild plants, including grasses and perennials like ox-eye daisies, sage, goatsbeard, lupins and ragged robin or cuckoo flower. These will come to dominate the meadow in later years.

Mow the meadow after the main flowering period (but no later than August) to give some light to the leaf rosettes of the perennials, so they don't rot. Mow again before winter sets in: cut it short now, and the mice and voles won't find much cover to hide in!

Before sowing, clear the area of roots and stones, and smooth it out with a wooden rake. Use

a mixture of grass and wild flower seed, and broadcast the fine seeds very thinly — about ¼ oz per sq yd (6–10 g/m²). A lawn mixture can be sown more densely — ½–1 oz per sq yd (15–40 g/m²) depending on the mixture you use. It's not always possible to sow evenly in one go. One way to overcome this problem is to sow half the seed in one direction and repeat the process with the other half at right angles to the first sowing.

Finally press in the seed with a roller, or by treading over the whole area with your boots. Alternatively you might prefer raking the surface gently to combine the seeds with the soil.

Keep the bed continuously and evenly moist for the next three weeks until the seeds start to sprout — and with any luck success will be yours.

39

Sowing your own perennials

If you want your garden to look really natural, you'll probably prefer to use native perennial species.

Most of these are readily available as seeds, but you may find ready-grown specimens rather harder to get your hands on. In any case, full-grown plants generally cost rather more, and it's expensive enough to lay out a garden without incurring unnecessary additional costs.

Sowing your own plants can be an advantage with bulb flowers or even ornamental perennials, especially as there are more and more new perennial varieties that will flower in the first year after sowing — delphiniums, balloon flowers and perennial lobelias, to name but a few.

This, of course, makes gardening much more interesting. Most perennials can be grown with a good deal less effort than annuals or biennials. In later years you can sow them again, or plant them out in beds. However, you will need to sow earlier — in February or March — and that means taking a few other appropriate measures at the same time.

Most perennials do well in porous, sterile seed compost, but they germinate less readily and less regularly than annuals.

You should always label each sowing, and transfer the label with each plant until it is planted out in its final position. You'll often find that you finish up using only a few of the plants, in which case labelling is even more important.

Cold germinators

Many perennials originally came from mountainous regions, and they have developed a foolproof way of avoiding premature germination in the autumn. Their seeds are inhibited from germinating until rain or snow, combined with cold, near-freezing temperatures, removes the inhibiting factor.

Most perennial flowers can be grown from seed.

A cottage garden can be a sea of colour from spring through to autumn.

Such plants include monkshood (*Aconitum*), spring adonis (*Adonis vernalis*), Christmas rose (*Helleborus niger*), lady's mantle (*Alchemilla*), pasque flower (*Pulsatilla*), gentian, various *Primula* species, globeflower (*Trollius*), violet (*Viola*), rue (*Ruta*), scabious (*Knautia*), heather (*Calluna*) and also many others.

These plants don't necessarily need frost in order to germinate, but they do need a period when temperatures are between 32°F (0°C) and 41°F (5°C).

If you want to sow them in the open air, the following method is the best. In the autumn or winter take a tray of seed, water it and cover it with a plastic hood or transparent film to stop the seed drying out. Keep the tray under a bush or in the shade of a wall so it remains at outdoor temperatures.

The cold treatment can also be carried out in a refrigerator. Keep the seed at 36–41°F (2–5°C) for two to three weeks. Then warm it up slowly so it can germinate, first at 50°F (10°C) and later at 59°F (15°C). Don't try to do this in a freezer: it's completely unsuitable, because it's designed to freeze things very quickly, and it works far too fast for the seed to adjust to the change in temperature. Even the hardiest seeds will freeze and die.

Perennials that flower in the first year after sowing:

- *Achillea millefolium* (milfoil or yarrow)

- *Agastache mexicana* (a giant hyssop)

- *Anthemis tinctoria* (dyer's chamomile)

- *Asclepias currassavica* (a milkweed)

- *Campanula carpatica* (a popular bellflower)

- *Centranthus coccineus ruber*

- *Coreopsis grandiflora* (a tickseed)

- *Delphinium* varieties

- *Dendranthema grandiflorum* (florist's chrysanthemum)

- *Dianthus barbatus* (sweet William)

- *Echinacea purpurea* (purple coneflower)

- *Lathyrus latifolius* (a perennial sweet pea)

- *Lavatera thuringiaca* varieties

- *Leucanthemum × superbum* (shasta daisy)

- *Lobelia speciosa* varieties

- *Lychnis × haageana* varieties

- *Lythrum salicaria* (purple loosestrife)

- *Platycodon grandiflorus* (a kind of balloon flower)

- *Rehmannia angulata* (Chinese foxglove)

- *Rudbeckia fulgida* (black-eyed Susan)

- *Viola cornuta* varieties (horned violet)

Seed table for perennials

Plant	sowing months	germination temp. °F (°C)	germina- tion period	where?	viability years
Achillea tomentosa (woolly yarrow)	4-7	54-64 (12-18)	30 days	gf	3-4
Aconitum napellus (monkshood)	10-2	32-68 (0-20)*	1 winter	gf	2-3
Adonis vernalis (spring adonis)	6-8	32-68 (0-20)*	1 winter	gf	2-3
Alchemilla mollis (lady's mantle)	10-2	32-68 (0-20)*	1 winter	gf	3-4
Alyssum saxatile (gold dust)	6-8	64-77 (18-25)	15-25 days	gf	3-4
Aquilegia vulgaris (granny's bonnets)	4-8	59-68 (15-20)	15-30 days	gf	3-4
Armeria maritima (sea pink)	5-6	59-68 (15-20)	15-20 days	sd	2-3
Arnica alpina	10-2	32-68 (0-20)*	1 winter	gf	2-3
Arabis caucasica	7-8	59-72 (15-22)	15-30 days	gf	3-4
Aster alpinus	5-7	50-72 (10-22)	15-25 days	gf	3-4
Astrantia major (masterwort)	10-2	32-68 (0-20)*	1 winter	gf, gr	2-3
Aubrieta leichlinii	5-7	59-72 (15-22)	15-30 days	gf	2-3
Campanula carpatica	5-7	54-68 (12-20)	20-30 days	gf	2-3
Carlina acaulis (alpine thistle)	3-4	54-64 (12-18)†	15-20 days	gf	2-3
Centaurea montana	6-7	64-72 (18-22)†	15-20 days	gf	2-3
Centranthus ruber (red valerian)	4-5	64-68 (18-20)	15-20 days	gf	3-4
Leucanthemum maximum (shasta daisy)	5-6	54-68 (12-20)†	15-30 days	gf	3-4
Coreopsis grandiflora	6-7	59-68 (15-20)	15-20 days	gf	3-4
Delphinium cultorum	3-6	54-64 (12-18)	15-25 days	gf	3-4
Dianthus caryophyllus (carnation)	3-5	54-64 (12-18)	15-25 days	gf	2-3
Dicentra spectabilis (bleeding heart)	8-2	32-68 (0-20)*	1 winter	gf	1-2
Dictamnus albus (burning bush)	4-5	54-59 (12-15)	15-25 days	gf	1-2
Doronicum orientale	4-5	50-68 (10-20)	15-25 days	gf	2-3
Echinops ritro (globe thistle)	4-6	54-64 (12-18)	15-25 days	gf	2-3
Gaillardia aristata (blanket flower)	4-7	64-77 (18-25)	18-25 days	gf	2-3
Gentiana acaulis (trumpet gentian)	10-2	32-68 (0-20)*	1 winter	gf	1-2
Geranium sanguineum (bloody cranesbill)	4-5	54-68 (12-20)	15-25 days	gf	2-3
Geum hybridum (avens)	4-5	54-64 (12-18)	20-30 days	gf	2-3
Gypsophila paniculata (baby's breath)	6-7	59-68 (15-20)	10-25 days	gf	2-3
Helenium autumnale (sneezeweed)	6-7	59-68 (15-20)	10-20 days	gf	2-3
Hemerocallis (daylily)	4-7	64-72 (18-22)	15-30 days	gf	2-3

* cold germinator; † needs light to germinate; **gf** garden frame; **sd** sow direct; **gr** greenhouse

Plant	sowing months	germination temp. °F (°C)	days for germination	where?	viability years
Hesperis matronalis (dame's violet)	6-7	54-64 (12-18)	10-30	gf, sd	2-3
Heuchera sanguinea (coral flower)	12-4	59-64 (15-18)	10-25	gf	2-3
Hibiscus moscheutos (mallow)	1-3	72-82 (22-28)	18-30	gr	3-4
Iberis sempervirens (candytuft)	3-5	59-64 (15-18)	15-25	gf	3-4
Inula ensifolia	5-7	59-68 (15-20)	15-25	gf	2-3
Jasione perennis (sheep's bit)	4-7	59-64 (15-18)	15-25	gf	2-3
Kniphofia uvaria (red-hot poker)	4-7	64-68 (18-20)	15-25	gf	3-4
Lathyrus latifolius (everlasting pea)	10-8/4-7	50-64 (10-18)*	120-150	gf	3-4
Leontopodium alpinum (edelweiss)	4-5	59-64 (15-18)	15-25	gf	2-3
Liatris spicata (gay feather)	4-7	64-72 (18-22)	20-30	gf	2-3
Lobelia fulgens	12-3	64-72 (18-22)	15-25	gr	2-3
Lupinus polyphyllus	5-7	59-68 (15-20)	15-25	gf	3-4
Lychnis chalcedonica (Jerusalem cross)	3-5	64-72 (18-22)	25-35	gf	2-3
Monarda didyma (bergamot)	3-6	59-72 (15-22)	25-35	gf	2-3
Oenothera missouriensis (evening primrose)	3-6	59-68 (15-20)	10-20	gf	3-4
Papaver orientale (oriental poppy)	3-6	50-68 (10-20)	15-25	gf	2-3
Pennisetum (fountain grass)	3-5	64-77 (18-25)	10-25	sd	2-3
Phlox paniculata	10-2	32-64 (0-18)*	30-100	sd	2-3
Physalis alkekengi (winter cherry)	10-2	32-64 (0-18)*	30-100	sd	2-3
Primula vulgaris (primrose)	3-6	50 (10), then 64 (18)	20-30	gf, sd	2-3
P. beesiana (candelabra primula)	10-2	32-64 (0-18)*	30-100	gf	2-3
P. veris (cowslip)	10-2	32-59 (0-15)*	30-100	gf, sd	2-3
Rudbeckia fulgida (black-eyed Susan)	3-6	59-64 (15-18)	15-25	gf	3-4
Salvia × *superba*	12-5	64-72 (18-22)	15-25	gf	3-4
Saxifraga × *arendsii* (mossy saxifrage)	3-7	59-64 (15-18)	15-25	gf, sd	2-3
Scabiosa caucasica	10-3	32-64 (0-18)*	30-90	gf	3-4
Thalictrum dipterocarpum (meadow rue)	10-2	32-59 (0-15)*	30-120	gf	2-3
Thymus serpyllum (wild thyme)	3-5	59-64 (15-18)	15-30	gf	2-3
Trollius ledebourii (globeflower)	10-2	32-59 (0-15)*	30-120	gf	2-3
Verbascum olympicum	5-6	59-68 (15-20)	15-25	gf	3-4
Viola cornuta (horned violet)	3-8	54-68 (12-20)	15-25	gf	3-4
Viola odorata (sweet violet)	8-2	32-59 (0-15)*	30-180	gf, sd	3-4

Houseplants and tub plants

Unusual or exotic plants are always a great pleasure, whether you've bought them, exchanged them, or brought them back from holiday. But some of these plants are quite difficult to propagate from cuttings — and in such cases you may do better if you try to grow them from seed.

Tub plants

Many beautiful tub plants can be propagated from seed in a pot, notably angel's trumpet, banana plant, *Jacaranda*, cabbage tree, bottlebrush, coffee bush, tree tomato, bird of paradise flower, oleander and various palms. They can be sown at any time of year, but need high temperatures (68-77°F; 20-25°C) to germinate. In winter (November–April) central heating can help produce the temperatures you need: that way there's no need for heated trays or germinators. Many tropical plants have hard-shelled seeds that don't stay capable of germinating for very long; try to use fresh seed.

File down palm seeds with sandpaper until the soft interior is just visible. Some seeds (e.g. coffee bush, coral tree, silky oak, angel's trumpet and ornamental asparagus) will germinate better if they are first soaked in lukewarm water.

With all these plants, it's important to measure the soil temperature, which can easily drop too low as a result of moisture evaporation or a cold window-sill.

Palms are generally slow-growing plants.

Houseplants

Spring is a good time to grow various exotic houseplants such as Cape primrose, flaming Katy, flame nettle, *Exacum*, *Gerbera*, *Fuchsia* or African violet.

Their seeds are very fine, and some are **photopositive** — i.e. they need light in order to germinate. Don't cover these with compost; just press them in, keep them moist and keep the air around them really humid (cover the pot with a plastic bag or a pane of glass).

The same goes even for cactuses, which germinate very fast and like a lot of moisture at first. Sieve some rough sand over them: this will give them access to plenty of oxygen and help to keep diseases away.

Ferns

Ferns propagate themselves by means of spores rather than seeds. In the case of most indoor ferns — bird's nest fern (*Asplenium nidus*), stag's horn fern (*Platycerium*), maidenhair fern (*Adiantum*) or sword fern (*Nephrolepis*) — you'll find the spores on the undersides of the leaves; on wild native ferns they form grey-brown stripes or spots. If you touch a fern, the spores fall off.

Take care to choose only perfect plants for propagating: deformities may be passed on. Germinating spores are vulnerable to attack by algae or fungi, so you should begin by sterilising the pan or pot, and the

compost, with boiling water. Sprinkle a few spores evenly over the surface of the compost. Label the plant, cover the pot with a sheet of glass, and stand it in a shady greenhouse or cold frame, or on a shady window-sill indoors.

Two or three months later the soil surface will become covered with a green 'moss' known

Tropical seeds being grown under transparent film.

as **prothalli**: the pre-germination stage. The male and female organs eventually form on this, and their union produces a new series of plantlets. Wait another 3–4 months until the plantlets are large enough to prick out into little pots.

Seed table for houseplants

Plants	sowing period	optimum germination temperature °F (°C)	germination period
Abutilon (flowering maple)	all year round	70-77 (21-25)	3-4 weeks
Acacia	all year round	72-77 (22-25)	3-5 weeks
Adenium (Desert rose)	all year round	64-72 (18-22)	1-2 weeks
Agapanthus (African lily)	all year round	59-64 (15-18)	1-3 months
Agave	all year round	54-64 (12-18)	1-3 months
Aloe	all year round	68-79 (20-26)	1-6 months
Alstroemeria	all year round	64-72 (18-22)	1-6 months
Anemone coronaria (crown anemone)	Feb.-Apr.	50-59 (10-15)	3-4 weeks
Aralia, Fatsia	all year round	64-72 (18-22)	2-4 weeks
Asparagus (ornamental asparagus)	all year round	72-75 (22-24)	4-7 weeks
Begonia	all year round	68-72 (20-22)	2-3 weeks
bromeliads	all year round	72-79 (22-26)	3-12 weeks
Browallia	Feb.-May	54-72 (12-22)	1-2 weeks
Calceolaria (slipperwort)	Aug.-Oct.	64-72 (18-22)	2-3 weeks
Callistemon (bottlebrush)	all year round	57-64 (14-18)	1-2 months
Campanula (bellflower)	Jan.-Mar.	59-64 (15-18)	2-3 weeks
Capsicum (ornamental pepper)	Jan.-Mar.	68-75 (20-24)	2-4 weeks
Cineraria	Jul.-Oct.	61-64 (16-18)	8-10 days
Clivia	all year round	77-86 (25-30)	1-3 weeks
Coleus (flame nettle)	all year round	68-75 (20-24)	2-3 weeks
Coffea (coffee bush)	all year round	77-82 (25-28)	6-8 weeks
Cyclamen	Nov.-Feb.	59-63 (15-17), not above 64 (18)	3-6 weeks
Cyperus (papyrus sedge)	all year round	68-77 (20-25)	3-4 weeks
Cyphomandra (tree tomato)	all year round	72-79 (22-26)	2-4 weeks
Datura	Jan.-May	68-75 (20-24)	2-6 weeks
Dracaena (dragon tree)	all year round	72-79 (22-26)	1-4 months
Erythrina (coral tree)	all year round	68-75 (20-24)	3-5 weeks
Eucalyptus (gum tree)	all year round	72-79 (22-26)	2-3 weeks
Exacum (Persian violet)	Dec.-May	64-72 (18-22)	2-3 weeks

compost	special observations
sandy	germinates easily but irregularly
sandy	presoak for 4-6 hours in lukewarm water, or blanch
sandy	fine seed: don't cover, just press in
sandy	large seed, irregular growth, place at ½-1-in (1-2-cm) intervals
sandy	germinates irregularly; treat like cacti
sandy	treat like cacti
humus-rich	presoak for 12 hours in warm water
porous, lime-rich	don't cover seed; pre-cool for 1 week at 39°F (4°C), then at 50-59°F 10-15°C)
peaty, open	only use fresh seed
humus-rich	presoak for 48 hours in lukewarm water; use fresh seed
humus-rich, porous	use sterile soil; don't cover seed, just press in; cover container with glass or film, and remove after germination
peaty on bark pieces	very fine seed: don't cover; keep continuously moist, spraying very finely
humus-rich	cover only lightly; prick out 4-5 weeks after germination 3-5 seedlings per pot
peaty, humus-rich	very fine seed, sensitive to fertiliser salts
sandy, on wet linen	very fine seed; keep moist and well ventilated
loamy, humus-rich	don't cover the fine seed; grow on in cool conditions
peaty, humus-rich	needs light to germinate: don't cover
very open, lime-rich	fine seed: cover only lightly; grow on in cool, bright conditions
loamy, humus-rich	only use fresh seed
peaty, humus-rich	very fine seed: don't cover
peaty (pH 5-5.5), very open	presoak for 48 hours in lukewarm water; slit or carefully remove husk; don't cover seed; always keep moist
peaty, very open	fresh seed dormant for three months; presoak for one day in lukewarm water; cover with ½-1 in (1.5-2 cm) compost; keep moist and shaded; after pricking out, grow on at 52-59°F (12-15°C)
humus-rich, open	very fine seed, don't cover, always keep wet
humus-rich, open	presoak for one day in lukewarm water
humus-rich	presoak seed for one or two days; germinates best in the pots of houseplants that are being regularly watered
sandy	germination delayed and irregular
humus-rich, loamy	presoak for one day
sandy	avoid stagnant wet conditions; pot in sandy soil
sandy, humus-rich	avoid stagnant wet conditions

Plants	sowing period	optimum germination temperature °F (°C)	germinatio period
Ficus (fig, rubber plant)	all year round	72-79 (22-26)	1-3 months
Fuchsia	Jan.-May	68-75 (20-24)	1-3 months
Gerbera	Jan.-May	72-75 (22-24)	2-4 weeks
Grevillea	all year round	68-75 (20-24)	3-6 weeks
Hibiscus	Feb.-Apr.	72-79 (22-26)	2-4 weeks
Hippeastrum (amaryllis)	all year round	68-77 (20-25)	3-10 weeks
Jacaranda	all year round	68-75 (20-24)	1-2 months
Jatropha	all year round	64-72 (18-22)	1-2 months
Kalanchoe (flaming Katy)	Jan.-May	64-72 (18-22)	2-3 weeks
Lagerstroemia (crape myrtle)	Dec.-Apr.	64-72 (18-22)	2-3 weeks
Luffa	Mar.-Apr.	72-75 (22-24)	8-16 days
Mimosa	all year round	68-72 (20-22)	2-3 weeks
Monstera (Swiss cheese plant)	all year round	72-77 (22-25)	2-3 weeks
Musa, Ensete (banana)	all year round	77-82 (25-28)	3-10 weeks
Nerium (oleander)	all year round	72-75 (22-24)	3-6 weeks
palms	all year round	77-82 (25-28)	1-6 months
Passiflora (passion flower)	all year round	72-82 (22-28)	1-12 month
Philodendron	all year round	72-81 (22-27)	2-12 weeks
Plumbago	all year round	68-75 (20-24)	3-4 weeks
Primula acaulis (primrose)	Mar.-Apr.	50 (10), later 64 (18)	3-4 weeks
P. malacoides, P. sinenis (fairy primrose)	Jun.-Jul.	59-64 (15-18)	9-15 days
Ranunculus (buttercup)	Sep.-Oct.	50-59 (10-15)	14-20 days
Schefflera	all year round	68-75 (20-24)	3-4 weeks
Schizanthus (butterfly flower)	Apr. or Oct.	61 (16)	2-3 weeks
Sinningia (gloxinia)	Dec.-Feb.	75-82 (24-28)	2-3 weeks
Smithiantha (gesneria)	Oct.-Apr.	72-75 (22-24)	2-3 weeks
Solanum	Feb.-Apr.	72-77 (22-25)	2-3 weeks
Streptocarpus (Cape primrose)	Jan.-Mar.	72-77 (22-25)	2-3 weeks
Strelitzia (bird of paradise flower)	all year round	72-79 (22-26)	1-6 months

compost	special observations
open, sandy	don't cover seed; keep well protected and lightly shaded
open, humus-rich	don't cover seed, keep moist and well protected
peaty, open, humus-rich	seed needs light to germinate; place sharp end of each seed in soil; keep moist but well ventilated
open, sandy	presoak seed for one day; cover with ½ in (1 cm) of soil
peaty, humus-rich	blanch seed with hot water or presoak for one day in lukewarm water
humus-rich	presoak for 2–3 hours; use fresh seed
sandy	presoak seed for one day
sandy, open	use porous soil; foliage lost during dormant period
open, humus-rich	shorten daylight hours and keep above 50°F (10°C) to stimulate flowering
loamy	needs lots of loam; don't let it dry out
humus-rich	likes high temperatures (77–86°F; 25–30°C) and regular feeding
humus-rich	best results from direct sowing, 3 seeds per 3-in (8-cm) pot
open, humus-rich	first leaves don't have any holes
peaty, humus-rich	only use fresh seed; file down seed husk, soften for 2–3 days in lukewarm water, or blanch with hot water
sandy	fine seed: cover only lightly; keep moist
humus-rich	never allow to dry out; roots often appear before shoots
sandy	germination very irregular; prune seedlings in winter to stimulate flowering
peaty, open	needs light to germinate and high humidity; germinates very irregularly
sandy	only cover seed very lightly with soil
peaty	don't cover seed, which is covered with an inhibiting substance; presoak for two hours before sowing
peaty	higher temperatures inhibit germination; always keep moist and shaded; sensitive to all but the weakest fertilisers
peaty, porous	don't cover seed; germination inhibited above 61°F (16°C); needs lots of nutrients; keep moist after pricking out, and grow on at 45–50°F (7–10°C)
humus-rich	a good bonsai plant
humus-rich	sow in autumn for winter cultivation; good summer flower too, but keep cool
peaty, open	cover fine seed very lightly or press in; needs lots of humidity
peaty, open	don't cover fine seed (needs light to germinate); keep moist
sandy	presoak seed for 2–3 hours; needs light to germinate
humus-rich	very fine seed needs light to germinate; press into soil and keep shaded
sandy	carefully remove seed husks, soak for two days in lukewarm water, and lay in damp sand; plant out after roots have developed

How plants can regenerate themselves asexually

Try a little experiment for yourself. Push a willow cane into the soil, and you'll witness a small miracle. Within a very short time it will take root, put out shoots, and hey presto, you've got a new plant!

It's not always as easy as that, because each plant species develops in its own particular way. But it's generally true to say that plants, unlike animals, have the capacity to reproduce

A new plant from every cell.

asexually from different parts of themselves, such as the shoots, roots, rhizomes, leaves and stems. This is an important way in which a plant species can regenerate in order to survive difficult times.

Gardeners have found various ways to use this ability, by discovering which part of each particular plant is most likely to grow successfully.

The most suitable 'parent plant' will be young and vigorous, and should still be in its full growth phase (i.e. before the seeds have started to form). Once a plant has seeded, it has fulfilled its reproductive function and begins to age. Warm temperatures also encourage cell formation — plants that are in their dormant phase are unlikely to regenerate successfully.

The parent plant must be well fed, and you must ensure it's free of pests and diseases. With some plants such as pinks, geraniums, chrysanthemums and strawberries, viruses are a big problem; they spread to all parts of the plant, and are carried on by vegetative propagation.

Tissue cultures

Viruses are one important reason why many plants these days are propagated in germ-free laboratory conditions from sterile, in-vitro meristem (growth-tissue) cultures. This propagation method uses a plant's ability to regenerate from even the smallest part, right down to the individual cell.

A sharp scalpel is used to cut out tiny sections of meristematic tissue — the only part of a plant that remains unaffected by viruses or bacteria. It can be found in various parts of the plant — the leaves or leaf stems, the root tips, tubers or flowers, or even the anthers and stigma.

These little cell groups are each kept in sterile conditions on a special nutrient-rich substrate. They grow quickly, forming a callus within three or four weeks and eventually putting out roots. At the same time they produce a whole series of germinating cells. These grow into new plantlets, which are later divided and separated, again in laboratory conditions. The most critical moment in the life of the tiny plantlets is when they are transferred from sterile laboratory conditions into ordinary soil.

Tissue cultures have become widespread as a method of plant propagation. Thanks to tissue cultures, many of the most beautiful and valuable orchids are now available at affordable prices. Many other plants are also propagated very effectively in this way, including lilies, roses, palms, perennials and ornamental shrubs. All the characteristics of the parent plant are carried on to its offspring, which are strictly speaking clones of the parent plant.

Unfortunately, the conditions necessary for tissue-culture propagation are very difficult to achieve outside a laboratory. So, for the time being at least, this method will remain the exclusive domain of professionals. We have therefore concentrated on the other main methods of vegetative propagation. All of them are described below, stage by stage, and with plenty of examples, so you shouldn't have too much difficulty in following them.

Propagation by cuttings

This is by far the commonest method of vegetative propagation. Suitable cuttings are taken from shoots or shoot tips and placed in a suitable rooting medium, which should be low in nutrients to encourage root development.

'Seed and cuttings' compost is widely available, or you can make your own rooting mixture out of one or two parts peat to one part sand. Many plants will root in an inert medium such as perlite, vermiculite, Leca granules or gravel — or even in a glass of water.

Most plants, however, demand little more effort on your part, and you will also need to know which parts of the plant will root most easily. This in turn will depend on the plant species — and sometimes even on the specific variety.

The most commonly used cuttings are **tip cuttings** — i.e. those taken from the tip of the

Many of these tub plants will root very easily.

main shoot or the side shoot. However, in the case of the Norfolk Island pine and some other conifers the side branches are programmed to grow horizontally, which means that any

plants derived from them will *also* grow horizontally. So all in all it's a matter of individual know-how.

A tip cutting should normally include three or four leaves or leaf pairs, and should be 1½-2½ in (4-6 cm) long and in its full growth phase (to ensure it contains active, divisible cells).

51

Take a sharp knife and make a cut immediately below a leaf node. The thickened plant tissue here contains lots of nutrients that the plant has stored up for the later development of side shoots, flowers and fruits.

The cutting will need to use all its available nutrients to survive the next few weeks, to close up the wound and to form the healthy callus tissue from which the roots can grow. You need to cut away anything that might hinder this process, such as flowers, buds or fruits.

If the leaves are very large, you should cut them down to minimise transpiration, and remove the lowest leaves completely.

Now plant the cutting about ½-1 in (1-2 cm) deep in a moist planting medium, press the soil in around it and water it thoroughly with a fine-rose watering can. Keep it in warm, humid conditions, and it will start to form roots.

Houseplants and tub plants

The simplest method: a cutting in a glass

This is an extremely simple method of propagating plants that take root very quickly. Suitable candidates for this include various shrubs such as forsythias and willows, and especially certain ornamentals such as oleander, busy Lizzie, ivy, philodendron and some begonias.

Example: *Begonia corallina*

If you take tip cuttings from a suitable begonia plant, they will readily take root at any time of year in a mixture of peat and sand, or in a glass of ordinary tap water:

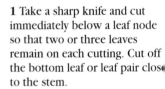

1 Take a sharp knife and cut immediately below a leaf node so that two or three leaves remain on each cutting. Cut off the bottom leaf or leaf pair close to the stem.

2 Place each cutting in a glass of water so that the wound remains submerged in the water; put a few small pieces of charcoal in the liquid to keep it sterile. Keep the cuttings at a high room temperature of 68-75°F (20-24°C).

3 Within about three or four weeks, you should find that the cuttings have developed roots. Now take the successful plantlets and put them in 4-4½-in (10-12-cm) pots filled with a humus-rich compost that is poor in nutrients. Water them well, and keep them shaded as you grow them on.

4 If you remove the side shoots as the plant develops, and stop it several times when it reaches a height of 12-16 in (30-40 cm), you can create an attractive mini-standard that will produce large clusters of pink flowers for most of the year.

Two of the five original leaves have been removed.

Other plants that can be propagated from a cutting in a glass

Begonia species

chandelier plant (*Bryophyllum*)

flame nettle (*Coleus*)

Dieffenbachia

devil's ivy (*Epipremnum*)

ivy (*Hedera*)

busy Lizzie (*Impatiens*)

flaming Katy (*Kalanchoe*)

oleander (*Nerium*)

Philodendron

Raphidophora

African violet (*Saintpaulia*)

Scaevola

house lime (*Sparmannia*)

spiderwort (*Tradescantia*)

Fast rooting in water.

Begonia corallina *is a good plant to grow from cuttings.*

Using soft tip cuttings

Many plant genera are characterised by soft leaves and relatively herbaceous growth, making them suitable for propagation by means of soft tip cuttings. In fact there are an enormous number of herbs, vegetables and ornamentals that will form roots from soft cuttings. It's hardly surprising, therefore, that this is probably the commonest method of vegetative propagation.

You take cuttings from some of the many shoot tips; each cutting should include three or four leaves or leaf pairs.

Using a well-sharpened knife or a razor-blade, take your cutting immediately below a leaf node. Try to work as quickly and cleanly as possible so as not to crush the plant cells. The smaller and cleaner the wound, the less likely it is to start rotting. Trim off the lower leaves: you'll find that this makes it easier to insert the cutting, and it will also reduce the area of transpiration.

Fill a seed tray or pot to the brim with seed and cuttings compost, or with equal amounts of moist peat and damp sand, and press it down gently with a piece of wood or the back of your hand to firm it. The mixture should be moist, well aerated, high in humus and low in nutrients — just the right combination for good root development.

As most of your cuttings are soft, you'll need to take a few simple precautions to stop them getting bruised or broken. For instance, you can use a small stick to make a planting hole about ¼-½ in (0.5-1 cm) deep, or perhaps 1 in (2 cm) for a larger plant.

Cuttings from geraniums, crown of thorns, cacti and other succulents tend to rot rather easily. They'll have a better chance of rooting successfully if you leave the wound to dry off in the air for half a day before you plant the cutting.

Example: fuchsias

1 This doesn't, however, apply to fuchsia cuttings, which tend to wilt very fast. With these you should work quickly and efficiently, planting them as soon as you possibly can. Remove any buds from the leaf stems, as these may interfere with rooting.

2 Insert the cuttings just over 1 in (about 3 cm) apart in the rooting compost, pressing it in gently around each cutting to make it firm. Water thoroughly immediately afterwards with a fine-rose watering can.

3 For the next three or four weeks — i.e. while the roots are forming — the cuttings must never be allowed to wilt. Ideally they should be kept in a well-sheltered location with no draughts and plenty of humidity. If you have no greenhouse, then a small home propagator in the form of a tray with a clear plastic hood will do as well.

We have found that transparent film stretched across the top of the pot is also very successful in keeping the air humid around the cuttings — or you could put the whole lot into a large, clean plastic bag. Stab a few small holes in the plastic or film to provide a little ventilation.

Otherwise this method requires very little effort, and the cuttings won't normally need any more water until they have rooted.

4 Fuchsias will root very quickly in a well-lit position out of the sun, and at a temperature of 72-75°F (22-24°C). You probably won't need to do any watering until the first time you check to see if the cuttings have taken root.

5 Provided enough roots have formed, you can then prick out the new plantlets into a suitable planting compost that contains a small amount of nutrients.

This lovely fuchsia will take root within three to four weeks.

Other suitable plants

Houseplants and window-box plants:

flowering maple (*Abutilon*)

Acalypha

hot-water plant (*Achimenes*)

floss flower (*Ageratum*)

Alternanthera

Ampelopsis

Norfolk Island pine (*Araucaria*) — only from vertical shoots

Argyranthemum

milkweed (*Asclepias*)

Begonia species

shrimp plant (*Beloperone*)

Bidens

Swan River daisy (*Brachycome*)

Catharanthus

slipperwort (*Calceolaria*)

bellflower (*Campanula*)

flame nettle (*Coleus*)

grape ivy (*Cissus*)

cigar plant (*Cuphea*)

twinspur (*Diascia*)

Gazania

ivy (*Hedera*)

heliotrope (*Heliotropium*)

rose of China (*Hibiscus*)

busy Lizzie (*Impatiens*)

jasmine (*Jasminum*)

flaming Katy (*Kalanchoe*)

Lantana

lion's ear (*Leonotis*)

loosestrife (*Lysimachia*)

oleander (*Nerium*)

Osteospermum

geranium (*Pelargonium*)

Peperomia

trailing petunia (*Petunia*)

Philodendron

artillery plant (*Pilea*)

Swedish ivy (*Plectranthus*)

leadwort (*Plumbago*)

Schefflera

Scaevola

Senecio

house lime (*Sparmannia*)

glory bush (*Tibouchina*)

spiderwort (*Tradescantia*)

vervain (*Verbena*)

Shrubs and perennials:

madwort (*Alyssum*)

Ceanothus

red valerian (*Centranthus*)

Cerastium

florist's chrysanthemum (*Dendranthema*)

Delphinium

fleabane (*Erigeron*)

gentian (*Gentiana*)

water avens (*Geum*)

Gypsophila

Heuchera

sneezeweed (*Helenium*)

rock rose (*Helianthemum*)

Heliopsis

water violet (*Hottonia*)

yellow archangel (*Lamiastrum*)

Lewisia

purple loosestrife (*Lythrum*)

mint (*Mentha*)

Monarda

catmint (*Nepeta*)

evening primrose (*Oenothera*)

knotweed (*Polygonum*)

Potentilla

azalea (*Rhododendron simsii*)

coneflower (*Rudbeckia*)

soapwort (*Saponaria*)

scabious (*Scabius*)

stonecrop (*Sedum*)

periwinkle (*Vinca*)

Herbs:

basil

chamomile

hyssop

lavender

lemon balm

oregano

rue

sage

southernwood

tarragon

thyme

watercress

winter savory

Hydrangeas are among the many ornamental shrubs that can be propagated by means of semi-ripe cuttings.

Semi-ripe cuttings

Many species can be grown from relatively soft tissue, and for that reason will root very readily. But there are other plants that call for a good deal more skill on the part of the gardener.

The majority of them are exotic tub plants, but they also include a number of ornamental shrubs. Because these plants are exposed to strong light and hot summers in their native countries, they have developed hard leaves and shoots to reduce transpiration and enable them to survive desert-like conditions.

Whereas ordinary soft tip cuttings are liable to rot, cuttings from these plants have great difficulty in rooting at all. The shoot tips take an extremely long time to root, and must be kept in humid conditions for months on end.

Commercial nurseries install mist propagation units for this purpose, using high-pressure sprays. This ensures that the plants are always kept in stress-free conditions that enable them to root fairly quickly with no danger of rotting.

Millions of plantlets are created in greenhouses and garden frames by this method, and a similar set-up is possible even for amateur gardeners (though they will need plenty of skill and experience).

However, most people will have to make do with keeping their cuttings in a box covered with stretched plastic film. If you water them with sparkling mineral water, this will help them to root and assist their later growth. So will a little fertiliser.

As an alternative rooting medium, you might try cubes of porous, airy rock wool and a rooting hormone to speed up the rooting process. This should ensure successful propagation of semi-ripe cuttings.

Semi-ripe cuttings, also known as semi-hardwood cuttings, are taken in summer from current-year side shoots that are just beginning to firm up and brown at the base.

This is a popular way of propagating trees and shrubs. Cuttings from deciduous trees are normally taken between mid-June and August; evergreens root better in September or October.

To see if your chosen shoot is ready, bend it between your fingers. If it breaks, the shoot is either too soft or too hard. If it's pliable, and springs back when you let go, the shoot is at the right stage.

Example: hydrangeas

It's fairly easy to propagate hydrangeas from semi-ripe cuttings taken in June, July or August.

Take 4-in (10-cm) semi-ripe cuttings anywhere along the stem (below or between leaf joints). Tug the shoot off the stem and pare back the tag of bark. Trim down to two or four leaves.

Dip the trimmed end in hormone rooting powder, liquid or gel, shaking off any excess.

Insert the cuttings to half their length, six to a 4-in (10-cm) pot containing either a commercial cuttings compost or equal parts of peat and sand mixed.

4 Water thoroughly with a fine-rose can. Then cover with a propagator top, or enclose each pot in an inflated plastic bag supported by sticks or a wire hoop and sealed with an elastic band around the rim.

5 Leave the pots in a warm, lightly shaded position in a greenhouse or frame, or on a window-sill indoors.

6 The cuttings should root in a few weeks, and can then be removed, but they'll need to be overwintered in a greenhouse or frame and transplanted the following spring.

This is how the Italians do it — air layering with the help of some old marmalade tins.

Other suitable plants

Tub plants:
Bougainvillea
Choisya
fig (*Ficus*)
strawberry tree (*Arbutus*)

Fruit:
blackberry (*Rubus*)
kiwi fruit (*Actinidia*)

Ornamental shrubs:
azaleas
box (*Buxus*)
Cotoneaster
Deutzia
Forsythia
rhododendrons
roses (species and old-
    fashioned varieties)
Wisteria
yew (*Taxus*)

Leaf cuttings

The begonias, in particular, can be propagated by some of the most extraordinary means.

Attractive foliage plants like *Begonia rex* or the expressive iron cross begonia (*B. masoniana*) can regenerate from only a tiny piece of leaf, provided some of the sensitive leaf veins are retained and are actually cut by a wound.

Propagation is only possible with fully mature leaves that have not hardened up, and that can survive high humidity and temperatures of 77-79°F (25-26°C).

There are several different methods of leaf propagation, including those using the leaf stems, leaf embryos and various sections of a leaf. One popular method for begonias is to use a whole leaf.

Example: begonias

1 Take a mature, healthy leaf from a *Begonia rex*, *B. masoniana* or eyelash begonia (*B. bowerae*). Put it on a cutting board with the vein structure facing downwards, and make cuts with a sharp knife or razor-blade at points where the leaf veins divide.

Keep the leaf intact apart from these cuts, and lay it on a moist rooting medium (a cleanly prepared mixture of peat and sand) with the vein structure in firm contact with the compost.

2 Weight the leaf with small stones to keep the wounds in full contact with the rooting compost. Keep the air humid (using transparent film or a piece of glass), and tiny new roots will start to appear where the leaf was cut.

3 Finally, take the leaf apart, and pot the tiny plantlets in a humus-rich soil.

Leaf-section cuttings

Plants such as the iron cross begonia (*B. masoniana*) and various leaf cacti can be propagated successfully from cuttings that consist of no more than a section of a leaf.

Again, the leaves that you choose must be healthy, and fully mature but not ageing.

Begonias propagate very readily from leaf cuttings.

Example: *B. masoniana*

1 Take a razor-blade or scalpel, and cut the leaves into rectangular sections about 1 in (2-3 cm) long, each with a number of veins.

2 Stand the leaf sections upright in the clean rooting medium (or you can simply lay them on top of it).

3 After a few weeks, roots and shoots will begin to appear, growing out of the wounds in the leaf sections.

If you prefer, you can cut the leaves up into triangular pieces, but you'll still need to make sure that each piece includes a cut vein.

Example: leaf succulents

In much the same way many succulent plants will produce roots, and later shoots as well, from their leaves.

1 Take a long, healthy leaf, and cut it up into pieces 1-2½ in (3-6 cm) long.

2 Leave the pieces out in the air for a few hours so the wounds dry out, then plant them in a tray full of rooting compost. Water them at once.

3 Keep them for three or four weeks in warm, humid conditions and they will start to form roots. Soon after that, shoots will begin to form along the sides of the cuttings.

With a large-leaved succulent such as this one, you can get lots of cuttings from just one leaf.

Other suitable plants

crown of thorns (*Euphorbia milii*)

mother-in-law's tongue (*Sanseveria*) — only the green varieties

Leaf-rib cuttings

A few plant species, especially those belonging to the Gesneriaceae (gloxinia family), have soft, fleshy leaves full of nutrients, and any wounds in the leaf veins and leaf ribs form a tremendous amount of callus tissue from which new plants can develop.

Example: Cape primrose

One very good example of leaf-rib propagation is relatively simple and produces lots of new plants — that of the Cape primrose (*Streptocarpus*).

1 Take a fully mature, downy leaf and a razor-blade, and cut the leaf veins along the sides of the central leaf rib.

2 The central leaf rib has now served its purpose and can be discarded.

Take the remaining two halves of the leaf, and insert each of them in a loose, damp mixture of peat and sand to a depth of approximately ½ in (1–1.5 cm), pressing the mixture firmly in around them.

Finally, take a fine-rose watering can, and water very carefully so the leaf sections don't topple

The Cape primrose is particularly easy to propagate from leaf-rib cuttings.

Keep the leaf sections in suitably humid conditions at an even temperature of 72-79°F (22-26°C). They will soon form tiny roots and a whole series of buds from which new plantlets will develop. To keep an even temperature you may find a propagator or soil-heating cables useful.

Wait for three or four weeks, by which time many plantlets will be visible, before dividing up the leaf and pricking them out.

Other suitable plants

gloxinia (*Sinningia*)
cardinal flower (*Rechsteineria*)

Leaf embryos

Leaf embryos — perfectly formed plantlets growing on leaves — are an oddity of nature. They occur on both wild and greenhouse ferns such as the appropriately named hen-and-chicken fern. But they're also found on vegetables such as tree onions, and on ornamentals such as the mother of thousands and its close relative *Kalanchoe laxiflora*.

The plantlets complete their full development while they are still a part of the parent plant, then eventually throw out roots and drop to the ground.

New plantlets appear on the leaf of a pick-a-back plant.

This process is particularly easy to see in the pick-a-back plant (*Tolmiea menziesii*), where the new plantlets form at the base of the yellow-and-green variegated leaves. You can remove the leaves at any time and put them in a pot full of sandy soil, weighting the leaf base if necessary. The plantlet will root after only a short time.

Other suitable plants

hen-and-chicken fern
  (*Asplenium bulbiferum*)
tree onion (*Allium cepa*
  var. *viviparum*)
Kalanchoe laxiflora
mother of thousands (*K. daigremontiana*)

Leaf-stem cuttings

Most plants that can be propagated from their leaves develop callus tissue on the surface of the leaf itself, but on some plants this tissue actually forms on the leaf stem, and it is here that the roots will eventually form. Sometimes it doesn't take any more than a few millimetres of stem to provide the necessary material for a new plantlet to develop.

The most suitable leaves for this purpose are those that have just reached their full maturity. At this stage they will still contain plenty of nutrients, and, just as importantly, their cells are still capable of regenerating. If the leaves are still too young, then they will be liable to rot.

61

Leaf-stem cuttings don't actually need much space for propagation, which is one of the things that makes this such a popular method among amateur gardeners.

Unfortunately there aren't many plants that are suited to this treament, but most of them are houseplants that can be propagated at any time of the year. They include both *Peperomia* and the popular African violet species *Saintpaulia ionantha*.

African violets are popular house-plants that come in lots of different colours.They are also extremely easy to propagate.

Example: African violet

Always use healthy, well-developed leaves from around the edge of the plant — they grow in a rosette-like pattern. These outer leaves are the most suitable; the ones in the middle can easily rot.

The plant doesn't seem to suffer when cuttings are taken from it. On the contrary, it almost appears to be rejuvenated by the process. If you divide the plant, using only one leaf rosette to each pot, and give it new soil, it will flower all the more luxuriantly.

1 First break off the fleshy leaves with their stalks, and shorten the stems to approximately 1 in (2-3 cm) using a good sharp knife.

2 Use a mixture of peat and sand, or a seed and cuttings compost; an African violet can even develop roots in a glass of pure water. Push the leaf stalks about ½ in (1 cm) into the soil, press it in around them and water them with a fine-rose watering can to bed them in. One technique we have found successful is to arrange the leaves in a circle around the edge of the pot.

3 In a greenhouse you can cover the pot with a thin layer of fleece — this will reduce evaporation and encourage root formation. In the home, a large plastic bag fixed over the pot should achieve much the same result, but don't forget to make a few holes in it to provide ventilation.

New life from old leaves.

4 Keep the pot at a temperature of 72–75°F (22–24°C), and roots will form on the callus tissue around the wounds within the space of two or three weeks. You can see this more clearly if you raise the cuttings very carefully. After another three or four weeks the first tiny leaves will appear.

5 When the plantlets are large enough, plant them out into well-fertilised, humus-rich soil. You'll have to wait a few months before the first flowers appear.

NB The plants will only flower profusely if they are made up of single rosettes. As each leaf stalk often forms a host of plantlets, it's best to divide these and plant them separately. You can even use the same leaf for propagating yet another generation of plants.

Other suitable plants

Begonia elatior

Lorraine begonia (*B.* × *cheimantha* 'Gloire de Lorraine')

sundew (*Drosera*)

orchid cactus (*Epiphyllum*)

flaming Katy (*Kalanchoe*)

Opuntia

Peperomia

hart's-tongue fern (*Phyllitis*)

Easter cactus (*Rhipsalidopsis*)

You can propagate roses from leaf-bud cuttings.

Propagation from leaf-bud cuttings

Trailing plants provide a large number of cuttings, and the same goes for plants such as roses that develop long, vigorous flowering shoots during the main growth season.

The nodes in these shoots contain a high concentration of nutrients ready for the development of new branches, and this can be put to work in the propagation of new plants. Although the tissue is already a little woody, it will readily regenerate to produce new roots and shoots.

Often the shoot tip is too young or too soft to be used. You'll have a better chance of success if you go further down the stem, and always take cuttings that include one leaf bud — or preferably two in the case of plants with paired leaves. The leaves are usually left on the cutting, though if you remove the lower leaf this will make it easier to plant the cutting.

Example: roses

By no means all roses are propagated by grafting. As well as sowing (in the case of wild species), it's also quite usual to use leaf-bud cuttings.

All container roses that are to be kept indoors are grown from their own roots, as are some open-air varieties that grow and flower better if they are propagated in this way.

Growing from cuttings also offers some advantages to amateur gardeners, because it means they can propagate a

articularly interesting variety
om a single parent bush.
However, there are often
otential disadvantages in the
ase of outdoor plants, because
ney may, as a result, be less
ost-hardy or grow less well on
ome garden soils.

Take a semi-ripe stem and
ivide it into sections. Each
ection should include either
ne or two leaf buds. Always
ut immediately below a leaf
ode.

Push each cutting about ½–1
(1–2 cm) into a container
lled with moist peat, or with a
nd-and-peat mixture. In the
ome it's better to use pots in
vhich one or more cuttings can
ke root and grow on undis-
rbed for some time.
Many varieties will root more
adily if you begin by dipping
e wound in some hormone
owder, tapping off the excess
leave just a trace.

Keep the cuttings in humid
onditions at a temperature of
2–75°F (22–24°C), and they
hould root very quickly. To
tain humidity, you could put a
ane of glass or some transpar-
nt film over the pot. For larger
umbers of cuttings, you could
se a propagator or a larger
onstruction with transparent
m.

After two or three weeks the
rst roots should have formed,
nd after a further two or three
veeks you can plant them out
a lightly fertilised planting
edium.

New roses from old

Other suitable plants
golden trumpet (*Allamanda*)
zebra plant (*Aphelandra*)
Aucuba
various *Begonia* species,
 including hanging begonias
bottlebrush (*Callistemon*)
Camellia
Clerodendrum
angel's trumpet (*Datura*)
Dipladenia
dragon tree (*Dracaena*)

rubber plant (*Ficus elastica*)
weeping fig (*F. benjamina*)
Gardenia
Hibiscus
wax plant (*Hoya*)
Lotus
passion flower (*Passiflora*)
Peperomia
Philodendron
string of beads (*Senecio
 rowleyanus*)
Stephanotis

Stem cuttings

This method can be used very successfully with houseplants that develop thick, fleshy stems. It's comparable with the use of hardwood cuttings for garden shrubs.

Stem cuttings are the solution you're looking for when the stem of a plant has long since lost all its leaves and its shoots have grown much too long. Such a plant is, in fact, in urgent need of pruning if it's going to regain the attractions it had to offer as a young plant.

The stem can be used to propagate a whole new generation of plants — and it's a method that works well with many plant species. With the palm lily (*Yucca*) it is so successful that the Hawaiians export pieces of stem sealed in tree wax (known as 'aloha-ti') all over the world.

Make a clean cut below a leaf node.

Stem cuttings root very quickly in the soil.

Example: *Dieffenbachia*

1 Take a sharp knife and divide the stem into pieces about 1 in (2–3 cm) long, cutting immediately below the leaf nodes. Make sure each piece includes a leaf bud.

Dieffenbachia can be propagated by means of stem cuttings.

Other suitable plants

shrub begonias (*Begonia*)
dragon tree (*Dracaena*)
Swiss cheese plant (*Monstera*)
Philodendron
palm lily (*Yucca*)

2 To prevent the pieces of stem from rotting, you should air them for several hours to dry out the wounds.

3 Push the pieces ½ in (1 cm) down into a mixture of equal portions of sand and peat. Water this thoroughly, and keep your cuttings in constantly humid conditions at a temperature of 72–79°F (22–26°C), either in a room or greenhouse.

4 The cuttings will normally take root very quickly. After th you can pot them and grow them on, keeping them in a warm environment.

Air layering

Air layering is another way of trimming down an overgrown houseplant so it regains its former beauty. This method is used for outdoor shrubs that form extensive roots, for house-plants that are too large to propagate in a propagation bed, and for those needing the high temperature and humidity available in a greenhouse.

Air layering also preserves the parent plant — but it does take a few months to achieve results. The idea is to stimulate the parent plant to develop roots from a wound in the middle of a stem. The upper stem is not completely cut away until the new roots have developed successfully.

In Mediterranean countries, air layering is a popular method of propagating citrus plants such as oranges, lemons and man-darins (see picture on page 57).

Example: Swiss cheese plant

Let's suppose your Swiss cheese plant (*Monstera deliciosa*) has an overgrown shoot that is in need of shortening:

1 Take a sharp knife and make a cut in the middle of the stem, immediately below a leaf node, *but only cutting half-way through the stem*. The plant continues to supply the whole

stem with nutrients, but a 'nutrient jam' occurs in the area around the wound.

2 Wrap some damp moss around the wound to encourage root formation, and wrap it in transparent film to keep the moisture in.

3 The new roots will take a few weeks or months to develop properly. When they have, you can safely remove and pot the upper section of the shoot. The parent plant will grow again.

Other suitable plants

shrub begonias (*Begonia*)

citrus plants (*Citrus*)

× *Fatshedera*

weeping fig (*Ficus benjamina*)

common fig (*F. carica*)

rubber plant (*F. elastica*)

Philodendron

other ornamental shrubs

Right Air layering is one way of rescuing an overgrown plant.

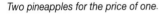
Two pineapples for the price of one.

Crown shoots

The pineapple (*Ananas comosus*) is one of the bromeliads, so it will readily propagate by means of plantlets that grow in the surrounding soil.

For centuries this plant has remained among the most popular of all exotics, with delicious aromatic fruits crowned by attractive crown shoots.

In the past, pineapples were a much-prized luxury among the nobility, and much skill and effort went into their propagation in the conservatories and orangeries of European palaces. Nowadays, with our modern centrally heated houses and warm greenhouses, there are very few problems involved in their propagation, though it is still a very slow process.

Example: pineapple

On the islands of Hawaii and Cyprus, and in many tropical countries, pineapples are a major crop, grown on large plantations laid out with yards of black plastic mulch. The crown shoots are removed from the fruit and pushed through cross-shaped holes in the mulch. They then root very quickly in the warm, humid conditions underneath.

At home you will have to use a rather different method:

1 Because pineapples need high temperatures, you can only propagate them when there is no risk of frost. Always try to buy the freshest fruit specimen you can, and one that hasn't suffered too much on its journey from the tropics. Carefully twist or cut off the crown shoot, and remove any flesh that is still attached to it.

2 When you remove the bottom leaves, the tiny roots on each crown shoot will already be visible. Put the crown shoots on a glass filled with water so that the roots dip into the water, and they'll continue to grow.

3 When the roots are about 2 in (5-6 cm) long, put the new plant in the smallest pot you can find (the ideal diameter is 3-3½ in; 8-9 cm) filled with humus-rich, organically fertilised soil on a drainage layer of sand or gravel. Keep it in bright, humid conditions at a temperature of 73-86°F (23-30°C), and it will soon grow on.

Leaf rosettes

Many houseplants, perennials and shrubs have distinctive leaf rosettes in the form of tight, flat clumps. One very good example of this is the group of grass-like plants known as the sedges (*Cyperus*), some of which can be highly decorative.

Example: sedges

The majority of sedges are particularly easy to propagate. All you need are some mature leaf rosettes and some glasses or bowls of water.

1 Take a leaf clump from a healthy parent plant, and shorten the stem to approximately ½ in (1-1.5 cm). If you wish, you can also shorten the leaf blades to make them more manageable.

2 If you put the clump in a bowl of water, it will quickly develop new roots and shoots in the middle; it doesn't actually matter which way up you put the clump. Within about three to four weeks the new roots will be ready to plant out.

If you prefer, you can simply put the leaf clump straight into a pot of moist rooting compost: the roots will grow just as well this way, and at the same time you'll spare yourself the trouble of planting out later.

NB The papyrus plant (*Cyperus papyrus*) is an attractive African sedge whose stems have a distinctively triangular cross-section. Since ancient times this

plant has been used for making papyrus, an early form of paper produced from the pith in the stems. The papyrus plant forms leaf rosettes just like the other sedges, but unfortunately these can't be used for propagation purposes.

Papyrus can, however, be propagated from the fine seed or from the fleshy rhizomes (see page 82).

These leaf rosettes from a sedge plant will soon grow on.

Bromeliad offsets develop roots while they're still on the parent plant.

Suckers

Many bromeliads, including the pineapple (see page 68), die very soon after they have flowered. Before they die, however, they provide for future generations by throwing out short suckers from which new plantlets emerge.

The same is true of the tropical orchids that (like many bromeliads) grow as epiphytes on branches or on other plants.

The roots form while the plantlet is still part of the parent plant. The more roots a plantlet has, the better its chances of growing and developing strongly. Choosing the right time for separating the plantlet from its parent is often a matter of fine judgement, and that comes only with experience.

With some plants the plantlet can be removed from its parent with nothing more than a sharp tug, while for others you'll need a good, sharp pair of secateurs.

Epiphytic orchids should be divided during the latter part of the dormant season, which will normally be in February. You can put the plantlets into fresh orchid compost straight away. After potting they will need slight shade, moderately moist compost, and plenty of warmth and humidity.

Example: *Guzmania*

Guzmania is a genus of long-flowering bromeliads that are both sturdy and attractive. Many *Guzmania* hybrids have beautiful, interestingly patterned leaves and bracts.

These plants propagate readily by means of numerous plantlets, which appear after flowering has finished and as the bracts begin to fade.

1 To remove each plantlet, grip it firmly and give it a sharp tug — but wait until a few roots have formed before you actually do this.

2 Prepare a fresh, porous epiphyte medium made up of loose, well-ventilated materials, and add a weak fertiliser solution. Insert the plantlets in small pots. They will soon form strong root balls, and eventually — after between 18 months and two years — they will start to produce flowers.

Other suitable plants

bromeliads — e.g. *Aechmea, Billbergia, Nidularium, Vriesea*

epiphytic orchids — e.g. *Cattleya, Epidendrum, Laelia*

Runners

Some houseplants develop long, arching runners from the leaf stems. New plantlets soon appear at the ends of these runners, which quickly form their own roots.

Perhaps the best-known example of this is the spider plant (*Chlorophytum comosum*), which forms little clumps of plantlets at the ends of 3-ft (1-m) long runners, giving the whole plant an attractive appearance.

The plantlets produce roots quite spontaneously. All you need to do is to remove them and pot them in loose, sandy soil with just a little organic fertiliser.

The spider plant is one of the most tolerant of all houseplants. It can manage on short supplies of light and warmth, and will also tolerate short periods of dryness. This makes it the ideal plant for a cool room or a conservatory.

Other suitable plants

flame violet (*Episcia*)

sword fern (*Nephrolepis*)

mother of thousands (*Saxifraga stolonifera*)

Offsets

Many succulent plants spread by means of strong side shoots known as **offsets**, which form

their own roots and leaves while they are still part of the parent plant. The result is a dense clump, which can be divided for the purposes of propagation.

You will find that large wounds are left where the offsets have been separated. These wounds are particularly vulnerable to the fungi that

cause rot, so it's important to let your offsets dry off thoroughly in the air before you pot them.

The houseleek (*Sempervivum*) is a good example of this form of propagation. The offsets form an attractive circle around the parent plant. All you have to do is remove the offsets, check that they have rooted and pot them in some suitably sandy soil.

Other suitable plants

cacti — e.g. *Chamaecereus*, *Mammilliaria*

other succulents — e.g. *Aloe, Crassula, Echeveria, Gasteria, Graptopetalum*

*Offsets from a spider plant (**left**) and a stonecrop (**below**)*

Only divide a slipper orchid if it's absolutely necessary.

Dividing houseplants

With many plant species it's easy to see when they're becoming too crowded in their pot, or forming too dense a clump, and dividing the plant is one way of dealing with the problem.

This is also one of the simplest methods of propagation, if not exactly the most productive. But the results are usually enough to meet the needs of a houseplant or tub-plant enthusiast.

African violets, bromeliads and orchids become increasingly tired with the passage of time, as they form bigger and bigger

clumps in the pot. They will thrive much better as houseplants if they are divided and repotted every 1–3 years (tub plants need a longer interval).

Example: slipper orchid

Slipper orchids (*Paphiopedilum*), like orchids in general, don't enjoy being disturbed, and will react badly to root damage. You should therefore only repot these when it's absolutely necessary.

1 Choose some suitable pots for the new plants. It's better if the pot is too small rather than too large. The roots will fill it faster, and it will also dry out more quickly after watering. (Orchid roots need plenty of air and react badly to stagnant wetness).

2 For this reason you should never use ordinary planting compost. Orchids need a highly porous, well-ventilated growing medium.

A suitable home-made orchid compost might include equal parts of coarse bark, fibrous peat, sphagnum moss and vermiculite or polystyrene chips

Alternatively, there are several proprietary orchid composts that you could buy.

3 Carefully remove the plant from its old pot, and gently shake off the soil without damaging the roots.

4 Tease the clump open gently with your hands. The roots should come apart naturally, and the plants will often separate quite easily. If necessary a

72

air of secateurs will assist in his process. Note that each new plant should have at least one budding shoot and a set of healthy roots.

Remove all damaged or rotting roots, cutting back into

lipper orchids are among the most beautiful of all houseplants.

healthy tissue so that rot cannot possibly spread. Hold the roots of each new plant in its new pot, and fill in the substrate around them, pressing down gently to make the plant firm.

6 Leave the pot in a semi-shaded position with plenty of humidity, and water it very sparingly until the new plant is firmly rooted.

Bromeliads and various other epiphytes — i.e. plants that live on trees without absorbing nutrients from them — need a similar kind of planting compost to orchids. On the other hand, they are capable of storing a little more moisture than orchids. So for these plants it would seem appropriate to use a mixture that contains somewhat more organic material.

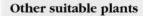

Other suitable plants

Orchids:

Cymbidium
Lycaste
pansy orchids (*Miltonia*)
Odontoglossum
× *Vuylstekeara*

Other houseplants:

African lily (*Agapanthus*)
flamingo flower (*Anthurium*)
ornamental asparagus
  (*Asparagus*)
cast iron plant (*Aspidistra*)
hard fern (*Blechnum*)
Calathea
papyrus (*Cyperus papyrus*)
cardamom (*Etettaria*)
Gerbera
sword fern (*Nephrolepis*)
African violet (*Saintpaulia*)
mother-in-law's tongue
  (*Sanseveria*)
clubrush (*Scirpus*)
mind your own business
  (*Soleirolia*)
Spathiphyllum
Cape primrose
  (*Streptocarpus*)
Zantedeschia

Outdoor plants

Natural layering

Some plants proliferate by means of a network of long runners that emerge from the tops of the roots. These runners spread in all directions, forming new plantlets with roots and shoots along the way. Later they break away from the parent plant and become independent. The result is a carpet of vegetation that covers the whole bed.

Propagating strawberries by means of natural layering.

Example: strawberry

The garden strawberry (*Fragaria × ananassa*) is a good example of this phenomenon, because it's important to keep the proliferation in check. Natural layering is a way of exploiting the process for the purposes of propagation.

The runners of different strawberry varieties grow in different ways. The number of new plantlets produced from a single parent plant can vary from 20 to as many as 100. With some of the sowing varieties, such as the

perpetual-fruiting F1 hybrid 'Sweetheart', the runners actually appear before the flowers. And even the so-called climbing forms produce long tendrils. In general, however, the runners don't appear until the fruits are harvested.

1 Before the new plants get a chance to take root, fill a whole series of 3–3½-in (7–9-mm) pots with a nutrient-rich planting compost, or garden soil improved with well-rotted manure.

2 You shouldn't have any trouble finding the nodes where the new plants will appear on the runners. Position one of the pots you've prepared under each of these nodes, and fix the runner over it by means of a stone or a wire peg.

3 Before long the new plant will take root and form a strong root ball in the pot. You can now remove the plant, in its pot, and plant it out in early to mid-August. You can expect a passable harvest from the following year onwards.

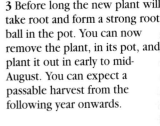

Other suitable plants

mock strawberry (*Duchesnea*)

ornamental strawberry (*Fragaria*)

yellow archangel (*Lamiastrum galeobdolon*)

water soldier (*Stratiotes*)

Dividing root tubers

Many plants are able to store large amounts of nutrients in a thickened part of the root called **tuber**.

However, not all such plants are suitable for division. Those that are have clusters of tubers, each with a developing shoot at the top. Strictly speaking these tubers are a thickening of the stem base where it meets the root. Plants such as ornamental asparagus have tubers that are actually part of the root itself, and are therefore useless for propagation.

Example: dahlias

Because dahlias (*Dahlia* varieties) were originally tropical plants, their flowers are particularly sensitive to frosts. So as soon as the first frosts have killed off the flowers — or perhaps even before that — you should cut down the stems to about a hand's breadth above the soil, and dig up the fleshy tubers as carefully as possible with a garden fork.

Put the tubers in an open plastic or paper bag, and store them away loosely for the winter in a cool, dry place (36-50°F; 2-10°C).

From March onwards, swelling buds at the necks of the tubers show that winter will soon be over. At this stage you should examine the tubers carefully, because torn-off roots will make them useless.

3 With a little twisting and turning, the tubers should come apart from the clusters, complete with the new plantlets. If you carefully cut each stem down the middle, you'll get two plants for the price of one. Plant out the new dahlia tubers in a sunny place in the garden in late April or early May.

NB Dahlias can also be propagated from cuttings, provided the shoots are still young and vigorous, and haven't become hollow. There also are a few varieties of dahlia that can be grown from seed.

Other suitable plants

glory lily (*Gloriosa*)
Incarvillea

Native orchids:

Dactylorhiza
Orchis

Only the budding tubers will grow shoots.

Dividing stem tubers

Some plants have a different form of tuber. It is formed by a section of the stem that has become swollen into an underground nutrient store known as a **stem tuber**. It enables the plant to survive the winter and to regenerate during the following spring.

Potatoes are probably the best-known example of stem tubers. Other plants with stem tubers include cyclamens and tuberous begonias.

If you look closely at a stem tuber, you will see the tiny eyes from which new shoots will eventually emerge — several from each eye in the case of potatoes. You can cut a stem tuber into pieces for propagation purposes, but each piece needs to have at least one eye.

Dividing tuberous begonias.

Example: tuberous begonia

1 Tuberous begonias (*Begonia* × *tuberhybrida*) are similar to dahlias in that the parts above ground die off with the first frosts. When this happens, you should dig up the tubers immediately, and overwinter them in a dry place, protected with peat, wood-wool or sawdust, at a temperature just above freezing point.

2 As early as February, new life will begin to stir in the tubers. Now's the time to brush them clean, bed them in moist peat or planting compost, and keep them at a temperature of

59-77°F (15-25°C). The new shoots will soon appear.

3 Take a sharp knife and cut the tubers into pieces, making sure that each piece includes at least one eye.

4 Plant the tuber sections in humus-rich soil, and they'll start to form roots and shoots. Flowering begins in May.

Other suitable plants

Vegetables:

Jerusalem artichokes (*Helianthus tuberosus*)

potatoes (*Solanum tuberosum*)

Houseplants:

angel's wings (*Caladium*)

rosary vine (*Ceropegia*)

Cyclamen

gloxinia (*Sinningia*)

cardinal flower (*Rechsteineria*)

Propagation from bulbs

Bulb plants play a very important role in the plant kingdom, and in particular in the world of gardening.

Botanically speaking, a bulb can be described as a kind of compressed underground stem. The leaves have turned into swollen, fleshy storage organs called **scales**, and are arranged concentrically around the compressed stem or **basal plate**.

There are two kinds of bulbs: **tunicate** bulbs such as those of narcissi, hyacinths and snowdrops, and **scaly** bulbs, including those of lilies.

As a bulb ripens, the outer skin becomes dry — later this will help to protect the bulb during its dormant winter period. The flower shoot for the following year starts to form inside the bulb as early as the summer (the ripening period) and autumn. New roots emerging from the basal plate show that the spring growth period has begun.

The bulbs of narcissi, hyacinths and various other genera develop **offsets** — small copies of themselves that grow around the sides of the parent bulb. If you score a cross pattern on the underside of such a bulb, this will stimulate the formation of small bulblets where the bulb scales are cut.

With hyacinths in particular you can produce quite a large number of bulblets by scooping out the bottom of the bulb after

Tulip bulbs will fall apart of their own accord, which is very convenient for propagating new flowers.

the growth season is over. If you bury these bulblets in peat or vermiculite, they'll develop into flowering bulbs within the space of two or three years.

Example: tulips

Look inside the brown outer casing of a tulip bulb, and you'll find not only the developing bulb for the following year, but also a series of bulblets that will produce flowers within the next two or three years.

These bulblets will need plenty of space and nutrients in order to develop, so it's a good idea to dig up your tulip bulbs after they've ripened, remove the bulblets and plant them (well spaced out) in a nutritious planting compost.

Never leave stands of tulips to look after themselves in poor,

sandy soil. They soon become exhausted, producing plenty of leaves but, alas, no flowers.

Wild tulip species such as *Tulipa sylvestris* will also propagate readily from seed. We recommend feeding them to improve flowering.

Other suitable plants

autumn crocus (*Colchicum*)

Propagation from bulb scales

With scaly bulbs, any scales that are broken off around the basal plate will quickly form bulblets. You can remove these as soon as they've rooted. Within two or three years they'll develop into bulbs capable of flowering, and you can grow them in the normal way. You will, of course, be able to produce more bulblets for future years.

Example: lilies

If you want to propagate lilies from scales on the bulb, one of your options is to dig them up during their dormant period. However, it's quicker and safer to remove the scales in the summer, keeping the bulbs on their sides in the pot or bed with just one side exposed above the soil.

Don't break off any more than three to five of the outer scales from each bulb, or you will risk weakening the plant. To avoid any danger of rotting, it's a good idea to dry out the wounds for several hours and then dust them with a suitable fungicide.

The callus tissue is going to need plenty of oxygen and high humidity levels in order to

Above *Lilies can be propagated by means of bulb scales, bulblets and bulbils.*

Below *Use a plastic bag to retain humidity.*

develop properly. One way of achieving this is to mix the bulb scales with sand, and then seal them inside a transparent plastic bag. A second method is to lay them out on a moist mixture of sand and peat, and then put a plastic bag over the pot to retain humidity.

It's very important to keep the temperature at the right levels, matching the changing needs of the plants. You'll want to maintain it at 72-75°F (22-24°C) for the first six to eight weeks; 63-64°F (17-18°C) for the subsequent four weeks; and 41-45°F (5-7°C) for the final twelve weeks. This 'cold treatment' will stimulate the formation of bulblets: do it during the winter in a slightly heated greenhouse or garden frame. Scatter the bulb scales over sandy soil, or push them in and cover them with ½-1 in (1-2 cm) of peat or loose soil.

The bulblets will form first, and in the spring they will be followed by the first tiny leaves. By the autumn the plantlets will have rooted, and the scales will wither and die. At this stage you can separate the new plants and plant them out into boxes of sandy soil.

Other suitable plants

fritillaries (*Fritillaria*)

Propagation from bulbils

Some lily species, notably the fire lily (*Lilium bulbiferum*), form tiny, bulb-like structures known as **bulbils** on their stems above the ground. These bulbils develop roots while they're still on the stem, and then fall to the ground.

The tiger lily (*L. lancifolium*) develops bulbils even before flowering has finished, and is closely followed by the fire lily. The bulbils will often grow roots and leaves, and fall to the ground, even before the growth period is over.

You can scatter the bulbils over a garden seedbed, covering them with a thin layer of sandy soil, or you can plant them in little pots. Another method is to lay the whole stem along the ground and cover it with soil so that only the tip is still visible.

Propagation from bulblets

Another group of lilies form bulblets along the underground part of the stem, just above the bulb. They include the Easter lily (*L. longiflorum*), the golden-rayed lily (*L. auratum*), *L. henryi*, *L. speciosum* and the subspecies *L. davidii wilmotti-e*. Between two and five bulblets are produced, and they normally appear in the autumn when the plant shoots have virtually died back.

If you dig up the bulbs care-fully, you can remove the bulb-lets and plant them in some porous, humus-rich soil. The first flowers may appear as early as the following summer, or during the summer after that. If you plant the bulbs very deep — say, 8-10 in (20-25 cm) below the surface — they'll almost certainly produce yet another set of bulblets.

Gathering bulbils from tiger lilies.

*Hot water plants (**above***) can be grown from scaly rhizomes (**right***).*

Scaly rhizomes

Some members of the Gesneriaceae, such as the hot water plant (*Achimenes*), have a rather unusual feature. When flowering comes to an end, they develop strange, underground swellings about ½-1 in (1-3 cm) long. These swellings, known as **scaly rhizomes**, are worm-like and creamy white in colour. As watering is reduced in the autumn and the plant shoots die back, these scaly organs continue to swell. If the plant is kept cool and dry, they will survive quite happily until the late winter.

Example: hot water plant

1 Take the plant out of its pot and examine the roots carefully; there should be several fragile rhizomes hidden among them.

2 Have some new pots ready, together with some suitably prepared planting compost. Ideally this should be a loose, porous mixture with plenty of humus and some organic fertiliser (bonemeal or a proprietary product). It's often a good idea to use a long-acting fertiliser that only releases its nutrients slowly. Each 3½-4-in (9-11-cm) pot should be able to accommodate between five and eight rhizomes.

3 Fill the pots up to within about 1 in (3 cm) of the rim, and lay the rhizomes on top of the soil. Add a further inch (2-3 cm) of planting compost and water the pots. Put them in a semi-shaded position and keep them at a temperature between 68°F (20°C) and 77°F (25°C).

4 The plants will soon begin to sprout, producing tiny, down-covered leaves. They will, however, react badly to cold water, developing ugly white marks on their leaves like other members of the Gesneriaceae. Their lovely flowers will appear in the summer between July and September. Many years of breeding have produced lots of different long-flowering varieties with blue, pink or carmine-red blooms.

Other suitable plants

Kohleria hybrids
Smithiantha hybrids

Propagation from corms

Botanically speaking, a **corm** is a storage organ formed by a compressed underground stem. From the outside a corm looks very much like a bulb, but in practice you will find that it develops in a slightly different way, forming several buds near the top. In due course one or more of these buds will sprout to form shoots with leaves and flowers, and eventually new corms will start to form underneath the soil.

Corm plants can also be propagated by means of **cormels** — lots of tiny offsets that can be removed just like bulbils or bulblets. If you overwinter these cormels and plant them out, you'll find that they will turn into flowering corms within two or three years.

Example: freesias

As soon as the first frosts are beginning to threaten, dig up the spent plants and cut off the leaves, leaving nothing but a short stump. Store the plants in a well-ventilated, frost-free location until a suitable day in the winter. In the meantime the plants should dry out, storing up winter reserves in their newly formed corms. Be sure to keep an eye on them for any signs of rot.

Before the new growth begins, give the plants a thorough cleaning. The new corm should look fresh and healthy in

Freesias produce lots of corms.

contrast to the shrivelled old corm left underneath. Now separate the two with a sharp twist, remove any old roots, and clean up the bottom of the new corm, where new roots should just be starting to appear. Finally you should twist off the old shoot, so that there's enough room for one of the buds to develop a new shoot.

3 Plant out the new corms in early or mid-May at a depth of approximately 2 in (5-6 cm). Ideally you should plant them in a sunny bed with good, humus-rich soil.

4 The numerous tiny cormels can be planted out separately. However, it has to be said that it's quite difficult to obtain successful results from freesia cormels.

Other suitable plants

Abyssinian gladiolus
 (*Acidanthera*)
montbretia (*Crocosmia*)

81

Propagation from rhizomes

Rhizomes consist of thickened shoots that grow horizontally beneath the soil. They are mainly filled with nutrients, and form branching structures with visible nodes, where roots and flowering shoots may eventually form. However, the final node at the tip of the rhizome is the main point from which flowers and fruits will develop.

Rhizomatous plants spread in clumps of varying density — some of them very slowly (e.g. asparagus and peonies), others much faster (e.g. couchgrass). As the rhizomes absorb nutrients, the centre of the clump eventually dies off and needs to be replaced.

If you're going to divide rhizomes, the ideal time to do it is during the plant's dormant period. In the case of plants such as Indian shot (*Canna*) this occurs during the winter. However, with various other species such as the common German flag (*Iris germanica*) it happens in the summer, after flowering. If you propagate the plant at this stage, it has plenty of time to take root, and you can be sure it will flower the following year.

Stands of irises will become exhausted after a few years.

You should take a sharp knife
nd cut 4-in (10-cm) long pieces
om the tips of the rhizomes,
hortening the leaves to a
and's breadth (i.e. about 7 in;
8 cm) in order to reduce tran-
piration. Treat the roots gently,
utting off any broken tips with
sharp knife.

*ke a rhizome with just one shoot,
d shorten the leaves to reduce
nspiration.*

To make the roots grow deep,
you should dig a circular trench
6–8 in (15–20 cm) deep and
spread the rhizome loosely
across the hump in the middle.
Pile some soil over it, press it
down and water it.

It's important for the tip of the
rhizome to be visible — it
should just be covered by a thin
layer of soil.

Loamy or mineral-rich soil is
much better for this purpose
than humus-rich peat. On the
other hand, too much garden
compost or other fertiliser can
cause the rhizomes to rot. They
will also root more quickly if
you plant them in a sunny
position.

Other suitable plants

Perennials:

sweet flag (*Acorus*)

Indian shot (*Canna*)

lily-of-the-valley
(*Convallaria*)

waterlily (*Nymphaea*)

pondlily (*Nuphar*)

Ornamentals:

mother-in-law's tongue
(*Sansevieria*)

ginger lily (*Hedychium*)

Cattleya and other epiphytic
orchids

Dividing up perennials

Clump-forming perennials can develop an amazing tendency to proliferate, sending out roots and shoots in all directions in their endless quest for new terrain and new sources of nutrients. In many species —

chrysanthemums, for example — the original plants will die back, so that the flowers effectively migrate across the garden.

There can be a number of possible reasons for this strange phenomenon. The plants may be attacked by nematodes, or affected by substances that they

themselves have produced — and sometimes they can simply use up all the available nutrient in the soil.

One consequence of this is that many perennials can often be rejuvenated by division. Indeed, where perennials have just such a tendency to die back, it's advisable to divide them every few years anyway.

The best time to do this is during their dormant period — say, on a frost-free day in late autumn or winter — or else in the early spring, before growth has properly begun. The weeks following the end of the growth period may also be suitable — for irises in July, after flowering has finished, and for peonies in the autumn, when growth has halted. Grasses should be divided in the early spring, because the plants are temporarily weakened by the process of division and may be killed by dryness or frost if they've been replanted in the autumn.

Dig up the roots, and divide them by hitting them sharply with the blade of your spade. Some perennial clumps are only loosely connected, and their roots tend to grow apart of their own accord; you should be able to tease them apart with your hands. Each of the divided plants should include at least one shoot and the roots that belong to it.

Colourful stands of black-eyed Susan.

Divide perennials during their dormant season.

general disturbance they will suffer as a result.

3 Cut back any damaged roots to encourage healthy regrowth, and place your newly divided plants in a carefully prepared planting medium enriched with humus or well-rotted garden compost. Plant them some 12 in (30 cm) apart, watering thoroughly immediately afterwards to bring the roots into close contact with the soil around.

Example: black-eyed Susan

Rudbeckia fulgida var. *sullivantii* is a variety of black-eyed Susan that comes from the Midwest of the United States. It is a particularly fast-spreading perennial that produces masses of flowers in the late summer and autumn.

The more familiar cultivar *R. f.* 'Goldsturm' grows to only 20 in (50 cm) in height, and produces single golden-coloured flowers that are dark brown in the middle; it is particularly suitable for borders or even containers.

Like all *Rudbeckia* species, black-eyed Susan grows in cushion-like clumps that flower less readily with the passage of time. It should therefore be divided every three or four years.

1 Divide *Rudbeckia* by April at the very latest, i.e. before the shoots begin to sprout. Dig deep with a spade to lift the clump out of the ground. Use the sharp blade of your spade to divide the roots up into much smaller clumps. You will probably damage some of the roots in the process.

2 As the clumps become more manageable, use your hands so as to minimise root damage. Try to divide them into sections measuring about 4 in (10 cm) in diameter, with shoots about 2-3 in (5-7 cm) long. The smallest viable unit is a single shoot with a bud and some roots. The less soil you have to shake off the roots, the faster you will be able to replant them and the less

Other suitable plants

Perennials:

monkshood (*Aconitum*)
Aster
florist's chrysanthemum
    (*Dendranthema*)
Delphinium
fleabane (*Erigeron*)
sea holly (*Eryngium*)
purple coneflower
    (*Echinacea*)

Herbs:

chives
hyssop
lavender
lemon balm
lovage
oregano
rue
sage
sorrel
southernwood
tarragon
thyme
valerian
winter savory
woodruff
wormwood

Propagation from hardwood cuttings

Hardwood cuttings are perhaps the commonest way of propagating shrubs.

Just put a few branches of pussy willow or forsythia in a vase, and watch how readily they put out roots. You can start off a willow fence or a willow arch by planting fully ripened one-year-old stems in the soil, and keeping them moist until they start to put out roots of their own accord.

Redcurrant, blackcurrant, raspberry, *Forsythia*, wild rose, *Philadelphus*, apple and grapevine are just a few of the many woody plants that can be successfully propagated by means of hardwood cuttings.

If you're looking for a large supply of cuttings, you can prune the parent plant severely the year before you need them: this will perform the additional function of stimulating it into vigorous new growth. However, most gardens will normally have at least a few plants that can provide the necessary young, woody stems.

Hardwood cuttings will quickly dry out and lose their ability to regenerate, so you should always try to use them as soon as you can. If you need to store

them for any length of time, you should put them in damp sand wrapped up in a moist cloth or a plastic bag, and make sure they are kept in a cool, sheltered place.

The best time to take cuttings is in late autumn after the leaves have fallen, or on frost-free days in winter. Each cutting you take should be about 8–12 in (20–30 cm) long and include several leaf nodes. At the bottom end make a diagonal cut immediately below a leaf node; at the top end make a horizontal cut.

Bury these cuttings in a deep, straight drill so that just the top two or three leaf nodes are visible. If the soil is kept moist, the cuttings will put out roots and shoots by the following spring. They can finally be planted out in the autumn.

In the case of roses you should look for fully ripened one-year-old shoots. These can be put into the drill as early as August.

Not all shrubs will root easily — in fact, you'll find that many of them won't take root at all. As with semi-ripe cuttings, it may be helpful to dip the wounds in hormone powder, tapping off the excess.

The grapevine is easy to propagate from hardwood cuttings.

Example: grapevine

You will find that just a few cuttings from a grapevine — or from any other ornamental shrub — can be quite adequately accommodated in a flower pot. You can propagate your cuttings in the open air, or if you have one available, they'll do well in a partially heated greenhouse.

Take your cuttings from well-ripened shoots on a frost-free day in winter. If it's at all possible you should try to use them immediately.

Each cutting should include at least two or three leaf nodes and should measure about 8-12 in (20-30 cm). Take care about the way you make the cuts. At the bottom you should make a diagonal cut directly below a leaf node, and at the top you should make a horizontal cut, just under 1 in (about 2 cm) above a leaf node.

Fill a flower pot with a mixture of moist sand and peat in equal proportions, and press the mixture down firmly.

Put the cuttings into the pot close together, pushing them in until just over 1 in (about 3 cm) of each cutting is buried in the substrate. Press it in firmly around them, and after that water your pot with a fine-rose watering can.

Now put a transparent plastic bag over the pot with two or three holes in it to provide some ventilation. Leave it in a greenhouse or in a shaded outdoor position, and the first leaves and shoots should start to appear by the next April.

3 In the early summer, transfer each developing plant to its own pot, and keep it there until you finally plant it out some time during the following spring.

Other suitable plants

Fruits:

bilberries

blackcurrants

gooseberries

raspberries

redcurrants

rootstock for fruit trees —
    e.g. apple, pear, plum etc.

Ornamental shrubs:

Buddleia

Philadelphus

and many others

The developing shoots on these vine cuttings are a sure sign of success. Commercial growers will soon go on to graft them.

Grafting

Grafting is a means of propagating plants that don't come true from seed, or that are difficult to propagate by cuttings, division or layering.

Put simply, grafting is the joining of a piece of the plant to be propagated — called the **scion** — to the rootstock of another plant — the **stock**. The two then grow together to form one plant. The stock provides the roots for the new plant, while the scion forms the part that flowers and fruits.

Although you can propagate a very large number of plants by grafting, in many cases it's quicker, easier and cheaper to increase your stock with seeds or cuttings. However, fruit trees are propagated by grafting, as well as some ornamental trees and shrubs.

The only tools you will need are a knife with a razor-sharp blade and raffia string to bind the grafts together. You can buy grafting wax or wound-sealant latex paint to make the joints airtight and keep out diseases — or you could use petroleum jelly. Adhesive tape can be used both as a tie and as a substitute for the wax.

There are many different grafting techniques — splice or whip grafting, whip-and-tongue grafting, crown grafting, saddle-and-bridge grafting. Each is slightly different, but the principles are the same.

Grafting is usually done in spring, just as growth begins.

Example: cacti

Many cacti don't come true from seed, and grafting is an easy way to propagate such plants. It can also be helpful with cacti that don't root very well, and with those that grow very slowly and will therefore take a long time to flower.

By grafting the cactus onto a taller base you may be able to persuade it to grow at up to twice its normal speed — and it's an invaluable technique for saving plants that have a damaged or diseased base.

Cacti are among the easiest of all plants to graft, and the best time to do this is in the spring or the summer. But it's essential

Cereus jamacaru, *like many other cacti, is relatively easy to propagate by grafting.*

columnar cacti, since these don produce many side shoots that might complicate the process.

2 Cut the chosen stock flat across the top at the point where the fresh, green shoot from the previous year began to grow — your cut should be within the top third of the plant, at a height of about 2 in (5 cm). To prevent any side shoots growing near the graft,

Roses, like many other garden shrubs, can be propagated by means of grafting.

le off the **areoles** — the little hoots from which the spines row — around the top of the tock. Clean and dry the knife fter every cut, disinfecting it vith a solution of alcohol. Now nake a similar-sized cut across ne base of the scion.

Bring the two cut surfaces nto direct contact. Press them ogether gently and turn the cion a little to remove any emaining air. Now secure them rmly together with two rubber ands, looping each of them nder the pot and over the top f the scion, at right angles to ne another.

Leave the pot in a warm, dry place that's not too sunny until the stock and the scion have joined firmly together. Water them very carefully for a couple of weeks, making sure that no water touches the actual graft point. When the fortnight is up, you should be able to take off the rubber bands.

Other suitable plants
Ornamental shrubs:
azalea (*Rhododendron simsii*)
Chinese witch hazel (*Hamamelis mollis*) on rootstock of *H. japonica* or *H. virginiana*
weeping birch varieties in winter on silver birch (*B. pendula*)
tree ivy (*Hedera arborescens*) on English ivy (*H. helix*)

Fruits:
apple, apricot, peach, pear, plum or sweet cherry on hawthorn, rowan or quince
fruiting walnut varieties on walnut species (*Juglans regia*)

89

Propagation from root cuttings

Perennials with thick, fleshy roots can often be propagated from root cuttings.

With most species this is only possible at certain specific times of year. However, there are just a few plants— horseradishes, for example — that will regenerate from root cuttings at any season. For other species, taking cuttings during the dormant winter period gives them the best chance of healing up their wounds and producing new shoot buds.

Early autumn, when the main growth period has just finished, is the time to prepare the parent plant so you can take root cuttings from it. Expose a few roots, shake the soil off them, and cut them off with a sharp slicing action near the neck of each root.

It's important for the new plant that you should know which end of the root is the top and which the bottom. As this isn't very obvious when the root has been cut, you should always cut the roots straight across at the top and diagonally at the bottom (if you have to shorten them) so as to avoid confusion.

Any fibrous side roots aren't much use, so you can remove them. The length of cutting you want depends on the level of nutrients the plant is likely to need to survive, and this in turn depends on the temperature.

The better the conditions, the faster the plant will develop an the fewer reserves it will need. A root cutting kept in a greenhouse at, for instance, 59-64°F (15-18°C) needs to be only 1-1½ in (3-4 cm) long, wherea a cutting left outdoors through the winter will have to be some 4½-6 in (12-15 cm) long.

Place the cuttings diagonally i a peaty soil mixture so the flat surface at the top is about ½ in (1 cm) below soil level. As soo as the new plantlets are proper ly under way, you can plant them out in little pots of planting compost or in outdoor bed

Remove the side roots of a horse-radish ...

xample: horseradish

hole fields of horseradish are own commercially, but just a w plants in the garden will be ple for any family's needs.

The horseradish has thick side ots about 6-8 in (15-20 cm) ng. These can be harvested at e same time as the main root the horseradish itself. Alter- tively you can collect them hen you dig up the main root smooth it off — a necessary ocedure for creating the vollen root that is used or sold ommercially.

Almost any part of the root ill grow on, but the best

section to use is a piece of side root about 6 in (15 cm) long. Remember to cut it straight across at the top and diagonally at the bottom.

You can either overwinter the cutting in soil under a garden frame, or plant it directly in the bed intended for it. If possible, choose a sandy soil that is nice and crumbly down to a consid- erable depth. Loam or clay soils tend to make harvesting very difficult.

Lay the roots in a deep drill, and cover them with soil to a depth of about ½ in (1 cm). Finally, don't forget to give them a good watering.

... and they will grow on as soon as you replant them.

Other suitable plants

Anchusa
carline thistle (*Carlina*)
knapweed (*Centaurea*)
globe thistle (*Echinops*)
sea holly (*Eryngium*)
meadowsweet (*Filipendula*)
cranesbill (*Geranium*)
poppy (*Papaver*)
pasque flower (*Pulsatilla*)
comfrey (*Symphytum*)

Propagation tables

Plant	Propagation method(s)	When?	See page
fir (*Abies*)	semi-ripe cuttings	7-9	56
maple (*Acer*)	air layering	6-10	67
hot water plant (*Achimenes*)	scaly rhizomes	11-4	80
	soft tip cuttings	5-7	53
	leaf-section cuttings	2-8	58
Aconitum	division	3-4/ 10-11	84
Acorus	rhizome division	3-4	82
kiwi fruit (*Actinidia*)	semi-ripe cuttings	6-7	56
floss flower (*Ageratum*)	soft tip cuttings	2-4	53
	seed	2-3	32
bugle (*Ajuga*)	natural layering	7-9	74
Aloe	offsets	5-9	71
Anemone × *hybrida*	root cuttings	9	90
flamingo flower (*Anthurium*)	division	3-7	72
Aphelandra	leaf-bud cuttings	3-8	64
apple	grafting	7-8	88
apricot	grafting	7-8	88
Araucaria	air layering	6-10	67
ornamental asparagus	division	2-11	72
Asplenium bulbiferum	leaf embryos	3-10	61
Aster	division	3-4/ 10-11	84
Astilbe	division	3-4/ 10-11	84
azalea	semi-ripe cuttings	7-8	56
Begonia	soft tip cuttings	2-10	52
	leaf cuttings	3-9	58
tuberous begonia	stem-tuber division	2-3	76
Bergenia	division	9-10	84
blackberry	semi-ripe cuttings	7-8	56
Brachycome	soft tip cuttings	2-7	53

Plant	Propagation method(s)	When?	See page
bromeliads	plantlets	all year	70
	seed	3-5	44
Brunfelsia	leaf-bud cuttings	3-8	64
Brunnera	division	9-12	84
	root cuttings	3-4	90
Buddleia	semi-ripe cuttings	7-8	56
box (*Buxus*)	semi-ripe cuttings	7-8	56
	hardwood cuttings	8-4	86
leaf cacti	leaf cuttings	all year	58
Caladium	stem-tuber division	2-3	76
bottlebrush (*Callistemon*)	tip cuttings	3-9	53
	seed	3	44
Camellia	leaf-section cuttings	8-9	58
	leaf-bud cuttings	8-9	64
	tip cuttings	6-7	56
Campanula	division	3-5/ 10-12	84
	soft tip cuttings	1-4	53
Canna	rhizome division	11-3	82
Centaurea	division	3-4/ 10-11	84
	root cuttings	10-12	90
rosary vine (*Ceropegia*)	rhizome division	all year	82
Chamaecyparis	semi-ripe cuttings	8-9	56
chives	division	11-4	84
	seed	4-8	28
spider plant (*Chlorophytum*)	plantlets	2-11	71
chrysanthemum	division	4-5	84
	soft tip cuttings	4-5	53
Citrus	air layering	2-11	67
Clematis	leaf-bud cuttings	4-10	64
Clivia	division	5-6	72
Colchicum	bulbs	6-9	77
comfrey	division	11-4	84
	root cuttings	3-6	90

lant	Propagation method(s)	When?	See page
ogwood (*Cornus*)	layering	6-9	67
	hardwood cuttings	10-3	86
azel (*Corylus*)	hardwood cuttings	10-3	86
noke tree (*Cotinus*)	hardwood cuttings	7-10	86
otoneaster	semi-ripe cuttings	5-9	56
rassula	offsets	5-9	71
ontbretia (*Crocosmia*)	corms	10-3	81
	cormels	2-4	81
edge (*Cyperus*)	leaf rosettes	4-8	69
ahlia	root-tuber division	11-4	75
	soft tip cuttings	3-4	53
elphinium	division	3-4/9-10	84
	seed	3	40
	soft tip cuttings	4	53
eutzia	semi-ripe cuttings	6-7	56
	hardwood cuttings	10-4	86
ieffenbachia	soft tip cuttings	2-6	53
	stem cuttings	all year	66
	air layering	2-9	67
ipladenia	leaf-bud cuttings	3-8	64
racaena	leaf-bud cuttings	3-8	64
	stem cuttings	all year	66
rosera	leaf cuttings	2-10	58
cheveria	offsets	5-9	71
	leaf cuttings	2-10	58
ater hyacinth (*Eichhornia*)	natural layering	7-9	74
pipremnum	tip cuttings	1-9	53
	leaf-bud cuttings	1-9	64
eath (*Erica*)	semi-ripe cuttings	7-8	56
rigeron	division	3-4/10-11	84
	soft tip cuttings	4	53
oral tree (*Erythrina*)	soft tip cuttings	4	53
rns	division	2-11	72
	spores	5-9	45

Plant	Propagation method(s)	When?	See page
fig (*Ficus*)	semi-ripe cuttings	1-11	56
	air layering	1-11	67
rubber plant (*Ficus elastica*)	soft tip cuttings	3-8	53
	leaf-bud cuttings	3-8	64
	air layering	2-10	67
Forsythia	semi-ripe cuttings	6-7	56
	hardwood cuttings	10-3	86
Freesia	corms	1-4	81
Fritillaria	bulb scales	9-10	77
Fuchsia	soft tip cuttings	2-7	53
Gaillardia	root cuttings	11	90
snowdrop (*Galanthus*)	bulbs	9-10	77
Gentiana	soft tip cuttings	9	53
Geranium	division	9-10	84
Gerbera	division	2-11	72
	seed	3-5	44
Gladiolus	corms	11-4	81
glory lily (*Gloriosa*)	root-tuber division	2-3	75
gooseberry	hardwood cuttings	10-3	86
	semi-ripe cuttings	7-8	56
Gypsophila paniculata	soft tip cuttings	5	53
	seed	3	40
	root cuttings	9-10	90
witch hazel (*Hamamelis*)	air layering	2-11	67
	hardwood cuttings	11-3	86
	grafting	2-3	88
ivy (*Hedera*)	soft tip cuttings	2-10	53
	leaf-bud cuttings	2-10	64
Helianthemum	soft tip cuttings	4	53
Heuchera	division	3-4/10-11	84
Hibiscus	soft tip cuttings	3-8	53
	leaf-bud cuttings	3-8	64
horseradish	root cuttings	3-4	90
hyacinth	bulbs	7-9	77
Hydrangea	semi-ripe cuttings	6-8	56
	hardwood cuttings	10-3	86

Plant	Propagation method(s)	When?	See page
hyssop	division	3-5	84
	soft tip cuttings	5-6	53
busy Lizzie (*Impatiens*)	soft tip cuttings	3-8	53
Iris	rhizome division	7-8	82
Siberian flag (*Iris sibirica*)	division	4	84
Jerusalem artichoke	stem-tuber division	1-4	76
flaming Katy (*Kalanchoe*)	soft tip cuttings	2-6	53
	leaf cuttings	2-10	58
Kalanchoe daigremontiana	leaf embryos	4-9	61
Kolkwitzia	semi-ripe cuttings	7-8	56
Lamiastrum	natural layering	6-8	74
	soft tip cuttings	7-8	53
Lantana	soft tip cuttings	2-8	53
lavender (*Lavandula*)	soft tip cuttings	5-7	53
	seed	4-6	28
Leucojum	bulbs	8-9	77
Lewisia	leaf cuttings	8-9	58
privet (*Ligustrum*)	semi-ripe cuttings	6-8	56
	hardwood cuttings	10-3	86
lilies (*Lilium*)	bulbs	9-11	77
	bulb scales	9-10	77
	bulbils	8-10	79
	bulblets	9-10	79
lovage	division	3-4	84
	seed	4-6	28
creeping Jenny (*Lysimachia*)	natural layering	5-8	74
purple loosestrife (*Lythrum*)	division	10-5	84
	soft tip cuttings	4-5	53
bergamot (*Monarda*)	division	3-4/ 11-12	84
Swiss cheese plant (*Monstera*)	air layering	2-11	67
	seed	3-6	44
mulberry (*Morus*)	semi-ripe cuttings	7-8	56
catmint (*Nepeta*)	soft tip cuttings	4	53

Plant	Propagation method(s)	When?	See page
sword fern (*Nephrolepis*)	division	2-10	72
oleander (*Nerium*)	tip cuttings	2-11	53
waterlily (*Nymphaea*)	rhizome division	3-4	82
water fringe (*Nymphoides*)	natural layering	7-8	74
tree onion	bulbils	6-8	79
Opuntia	leaf cuttings	2-10	58
orchids	division	2-8	72
oregano	division	3-5/ 9-11	84
	semi-ripe cuttings	5-7	56
poppy (*Papaver*)	root cuttings	9-10	90
slipper orchid (*Paphiopedilum*)	division	2-7	72
passion flower (*Passiflora*)	leaf-bud cuttings	3-8	64
peach	grafting	7-8	88
pear	grafting	7-8	88
Pelargonium	soft tip cuttings	3-7	53
Peperomia	soft tip cuttings	2-11	53
	leaf-stem cuttings	2-11	61
Philadelphus	hardwood cuttings	10-3	86
Philodendron	soft tip cuttings	3-7	53
	stem cuttings	2-11	66
	air layering	2-11	67
Phlox	division	3-4/ 10-11	84
	root cuttings	9	90
Phyllitis	division	4	72
Physalis	natural layering	7-9	74
spruce (*Picea*)	semi-ripe cuttings	8-9	56
pineapple	crown shoots	2-10	68
plum	hardwood cuttings	10-3	86
	grafting	3	88
Plumbago	soft tip cuttings	3-7	53
	seed	3-4	44

VEGETATIVE PROPAGATION

lant	Propagation method(s)	When?	See page
olygonum	tip cuttings	4	53
	natural layering	7-9	74
oplar (*Populus*)	hardwood cuttings	10-3	86
otamogeton	natural layering	6-8	74
rimula	division	10-11	84
enticulata	root cuttings	9	90
herry laurel	semi-ripe cuttings	8-9	56
Prunus laurocerasus)			
asque flower	root cuttings	11	90
Pulsatilla)			
yracantha	semi-ripe cuttings	7-8	56
aspberry	hardwood cuttings	10-3	86
rnamental	semi-ripe cuttings	6-7	56
urrant (*Ribes*)	hardwood cuttings	10-3	86
oses (*Rosa*)	hardwood cuttings	10-3	86
	leaf-bud cuttings	8	64
osemary	semi-ripe cuttings	4-7	56
oneflower	division	10-4	84
Rudbeckia)			
agittaria	natural layering	7-9	74
frican violet	division	2-11	72
Saintpaulia)	leaf-stem cuttings	2-11	61
villow (*Salix*)	hardwood cuttings	10-3	86
der (*Sambucus*)	semi-ripe cuttings	6-7	56
	hardwood cuttings	10-3	86
anseveria	rhizome division	2-10	82
	leaf-section cuttings	2-10	58
axifraga	plantlets	6-9	71
olonifera			
cabious	division	3-4	84
Scabiosa)			
onecrop	division	10-4	84
Sedum)	soft tip cuttings	4	53
ouseleek	offsets	5-8	71
Sempervivum)			
oxinia	stem-tuber division	2-3	76
inningia)	leaf-rib cuttings	2-9	60
kimmia	semi-ripe cuttings	7-8	56
	hardwood cuttings	10-3	86

Plant	Propagation method(s)	When?	See page
gesneria (*Smithiantha*)	scaly rhizomes	3-5	80
sorrel	division	4-5	84
	seed	4-8	28
Spiraea	semi-ripe cuttings	6-7	56
Stephanotis	leaf-bud cuttings	3-8	64
strawberry	natural layering	6-7	74
Cape primrose (*Streptocarpus*)	division	2-11	72
	leaf-rib cuttings	2-9	60
lilac (*Syringa*)	semi-ripe cuttings	7-8	56
	hardwood cuttings	10-3	86
tamarisk (*Tamarix*)	semi-ripe cuttings	7-8	56
	hardwood cuttings	9	86
tarragon	division	2-3	84
	soft tip cuttings	4-6	53
yew (*Taxus*)	semi-ripe cuttings	7-9	56
thyme (*Thymus*)	soft tip cuttings	5-7	53
	seed	3-4	28
foam flower (*Tiarella*)	division	3-4/ 10-11	84
pick-a-back plant (*Tolmiea*)	leaf embryos	4-10	61
hemlock (*Tsuga*)	semi-ripe cuttings	8-9	56
tulip (*Tulipa*)	bulbs	8-10	77
mullein (*Verbascum*)	root cuttings	9	90
	seed	3-5	40
Viburnum	hardwood cuttings	9	86
periwinkle (*Vinca*)	tip cuttings	7-8	53
grapevine (*Vitis*)	leaf-bud cuttings	7-8	64
	hardwood cuttings (under glass)	11-3	86
	grafting	1-3	88
walnut	grafting	3-4	88
Wisteria	semi-ripe cuttings	7-8	56
woodruff	division	6	84
wormwood	semi-ripe cuttings	7-8	56
Yucca	rhizome division	2-4	82
Zantedeschia	rhizome division	2-11	82

Index